Roadside Plants and Flowers

Roadside Plants and Flowers

*A Traveler's Guide
to the Midwest and
Great Lakes Area*

With a Few Familiar
Off-Road Wildflowers

Marian S. Edsall

The University of Wisconsin Press

A North Coast Book

The University of Wisconsin Press
2537 Daniels Street
Madison, Wisconsin 53718

3 Henrietta Street
London WC2E 8LU, England

Library of Congress Cataloging-in-Publication Data
Edsall, Marian S.
Roadside plants and flowers.
Bibliography: pp. 135–136.
Includes index.
1. Roadside flora—Middle West—Identification. 2. Roadside flora—
Great Lakes Region—Identification. 3. Wild flowers—Middle West—Identi-
fication. 4. Wild flowers—Great Lakes Region—Identification. I. Title.
QK128.E37 1984   582.0977   84-40148
ISBN 0-299-09700-5
ISBN 0-299-09704-8 (pbk.)

Contents

Foreword

MIDWESTERNERS HAVE a special fondness for the out-of-doors and the things that grow there. Our winters, often long and harsh, prepare us to feel a great relief and liberation when spring flowers around us, summer blooms, and autumn catches fire with color.

My family was one in which it was expected that we notice nature in detail. And so I did—in northern Michigan, where I grew up; in Illinois, where I studied; and in Wisconsin, where I have made a career and raised a family. For some years, when I was Wisconsin Secretary of Natural Resources, noticing and protecting nature was my mission.

Today, I put myself outdoors as often as I can. I run several miles daily, fish when I can, and travel widely over Wisconsin and across the Midwest to stay in touch with the citizens of Wisconsin and the governors of the Great Lakes states.

Marian Edsall's book is going to be my companion for some time to come. Experienced travelers know that it is one thing to tour and a better thing to get to know the inhabitants. *Roadside Plants and Flowers* gives us the chance to be more than tourists in our environment: it gives us the chance to peek into the lives of the plant communities and discover the local flowers.

This is a book that should be in the knapsack, picnic basket, and automobile glove compartment of every Midwesterner or traveler in the Midwest who plans to stop by a roadside or hike into a forest. Mrs. Edsall is a helpful guide and a clear writer. Her readers will not lose their way in the prairies or in her prose.

I expect that, like many of the flowers in these pages, *Roadside Plants and Flowers* will be a perennial favorite.

Anthony S. Earl
Governor of Wisconsin

Madison, June 1983

Introduction

HAVE YOU ever wondered about the bright orange flowers you see growing beside the highway, or the cluster of purple spires that caught your eye as you were traveling down the road? Depending on the season and the terrain, the flash of orange may have been Turk's Cap Lily, Hawkweed, or Butterfly Weed, the purple Blazing-Star, Fireweed, or Loosestrife, all colorful and interesting plants that you can readily see from your car window or from your bicycle.

Travelers on the freeways, highways, and byways of the Midwest and Great Lakes area pass a great variety of plant life on the right-of-ways, in ditches, and along fence rows. Many plants reveal their abundance amidst this roadside vegetation when they flower at some time during the growing season. Even the mowed expanses along four-lane super-highways sport patches of wildflowers that defy constant cutting. Learning to recognize them and learning something about them can add a new dimension to any trip, whether you are driving, biking, or hiking. Reading the landscape can be more interesting than reading billboards.

This guide to some of the common plants most apt to catch the eye and attention while traveling is a simple introduction in nontechnical terms to the fascinating world of wayside flowers and weeds.

What are these plants that have made themselves at home beside the concrete and gravel of highways, or have continued to thrive close by when man has cut a passageway through their woodland, marsh, or meadow habitats?

Weeds or Flowers?

One person's weed may be another's flower. One summer I had a pretty bouquet on a table at a country fair. A passing farmer snorted derisively, "Just a bunch of weeds!" Meanwhile, the town and city folk were "oh-ing" and "ah-ing" over the mixture of Queen Anne's Lace, Daisies, Bergamot, and Black-eyed Susans that I had picked beside the road.

The term *weed* has had many definitions, mainly derogatory. One dictionary dismisses it as "wild or obnoxious growth." Others apply the word to any plant that grows rapidly and abundantly where it is not wanted, more foe than friend. In the ecological sense, weeds are plants that grow fast, are mainly short-lived, and resist abuse. Or, as some say, "a plant out of place."

But who is to say that Boneset, Joe-Pye-Weed, or Evening Primrose, all of which appear in weed guides as well as in wildflower books, are "out of place"? Weeds are sometimes characterized as sun-loving plants of disturbed ground, but in that limited sense so, too, are farm crops and many of our garden flowers. Admittedly, some so-called weeds are truly pests to man—ragweed and thistles, for example. But even these have the redeeming feature of serving the needs of wildlife. Other unsightly or disliked intruders help to cover recently exposed or disturbed ground and to prevent erosion.

Many of the wayside plants in this book, whether you consider them weeds or flowers, are "aliens" in the botanical sense—another faintly disparaging term. That simply means that they are not native to North America, but are immigrants, primarily from the Old World, just as were the ancestors of most of us. They came as seed or plant stock brought in purposely or inadvertently by early settlers, or as stowaways in various shipments. Some escaped cultivation, and others, unnoticed, spread rapidly and sometimes aggressively in their new home. For this reason, they are often called "white man's plants."

A Rose by Any Other Name

Most plants have a common name; if they don't, it usually means that they are not very common or familiar. The plants in this book are first identified by their most widely used common name, plus any one or more of the colloquial variants by which they are known locally. The vernacular names are often descriptive, even poetic, and some have historic allusions, but there are drawbacks to this way of referring to them. The informal name may vary from one locale to another; the name may be misleading (Blue-eyed Grass, for example, is not a grass at all); and sometimes the same name is given to very different plants. I had several people in mid-Wisconsin insist that the Wild Columbine we were admiring was Honeysuckle, and that, apparently, was the traditional name used in the area, although most of us use these two common names for two dissimilar plants.

To avoid this confusion, botanists use scientific names based on a classification system so that every plant has a name which can be understood anywhere in the world. Plants that are related by sharing some common characteristics (not always visible or readily apparent) are classified into families. Families are subdivided into genera, plants with additional similarities. Particular kinds of plants within a genus are given species names; these terms further describe the plant in some special way. Thus our Wild Columbine is in the Buttercup family (Ranunculaceae), the genus is *Aquilegia,* and the species, *Aquilegia canadensis.* Honeysuckle belongs to a family (Caprifoliaceae) which includes flowering vines and shrubs in the genera *Lonicera* and *Diervilla.* In some cases, scientists do not agree on the particular species of some plants which have been hybridized (by cross-pollination between species) or which differ only in some obscure detail.

Family names are not indicated herein because they are not really very helpful to the novice. It is difficult, for example, to see the kinship between strawberries, apples, Cinquefoils, Steeplebush, and Meadowsweet, all of which are in the Rose family (Rosaceae); the family name is of little aid to initial recognition. However, the species name of each plant described in this book is included, following the common name(s), so that the plant can be identified and distinguished from its close relatives by reference to other, more detailed guides. (Occasionally only the genus name is given, followed by "sp.," indicating that the plant pictured could be any one of various species.)

Botanists also use some highly technical and unfamiliar terms to describe plants accurately; a few such words cannot be avoided, and you will find a list of those which are not self-evident in a short glossary that follows.

So much for nomenclature. You can begin to recognize some common plants without resorting to a lot of scientific terms. When curiosity and interest are aroused, you will want to go further afield and check the more exhaustive descriptions in other books; some of the more useful ones are listed in the bibliography. There is far more to the fascinating wild plant life about us than the splash of color or the odd design of these few.

When and Where to Look

A continuous pageant of bloom unfolds along the road from the first greening in spring to the final killing frost of late fall. Most flowers have a peak blooming season, a period when the majority of the plants of any one species in a given area is in full blossom. This time will vary somewhat from year to year, depending on temperature variations and the amount of sunlight and rain received. The same factors influence the abundance or lushness of growth of a particular species in any one year or in any one area; there are good years and bad years, especially for those plants which have specific needs at some critical period in their growth. Individual specimens of the same plant may vary from robust and healthy to straggly and stunted according to the soil conditions and orientation, even in adjacent areas.

Some blossoms last only a week or so, and the plants may disappear altogether or be overshadowed by later-growing or aggressive neighbors. Others will continue to blossom sporadically throughout the growing season, or persist conspicuously as they progress from flower to fruit.

The season noted in the following descriptions covers just about the maximum time you would expect to see the plant readily. The local blooming period within this time frame will depend not only on the climatic conditions of the year, but also on whether you are in a southern or northern portion of the geographical range covered (the dark area on the map). Although this guide is intended primarily for the Midwest and

Great Lakes area, almost all of these plants are wide-ranging wanderers and can be found further east and in the South as well, and many have traveled westward.

Finding these common wayside plants is a game of chance as you travel. From the car window I once counted twenty-five colorful flowering species along a short stretch of freeway. Then, abruptly, there was little more than the violet haze of masses of Spotted Knapweed lining the shoulders for miles.

Plants have definite habitat preferences, and our highways and byways cut through many types of terrain. The trained botanist will know and the observant novice will soon learn where to look for certain plants as the road passes from meadow to woodlot, cuts along hillsides and dips into valleys, skirts wetlands and bogs, traverses sand barrens, and runs along fallow fields. The best hunting is done on meandering back roads, but most of the plants in this book, native or alien, thrive in open areas or disturbed ground where they can be easily seen and recognized by general shape and color.

To Pick or Protect?

Some few of the flowers included here are endangered or fast disappearing because of overpicking or the destruction of habitat. Many states have enacted laws to protect them, making it illegal to pick, transport, or transplant them. On the other hand, attempts to control or eradicate roadside growth by spraying and indiscriminate mowing have discouraged some of our more colorful waysiders. Fortunately these destructive actions have been halted or reduced in many localities; the growing recognition of what we are losing has led to the development of highway beautification programs in some states. Garden clubs and highway departments have cooperated to sow wildflower seeds and transplant some specimens, and mowing is delayed until blossoms have faded and seeds are set. Occasionally, when grading is necessary through a stand of wildflowers, a layer of sod and topsoil is first removed, laid aside and watered until the work is finished, and then replaced. Many times these efforts have not only preserved or added to the beauty of the landscape, but have actually cut down on the cost of roadway maintenance.

The temptation to pick wildflowers is very human and natural, and many of the more aggressive ones can be gathered for a close-up delight in their color and beauty when this is done with care. Pick sparingly, and cut or break stems so that the plant is not uprooted. Leave woodland flowers for others to enjoy. If there are only a few specimens in a stand, take a picture, not a blossom. Learn to recognize protected and endangered plants, and encourage others to admire without disturbing. But enjoy a wild bouquet of Daisies, Buttercups, Black-eyed Susans, or Asters if you wish.

About This Guide

The plants described here are arranged according to the usual color of their blossoms or distinguishing features. The color variations that occur within some species are noted in the text. Occasionally two species in the same genus but of a different color are included together because you are apt to find them together. (At the beginning of the index, you will find a list of plants that are described elsewhere than in their own color sections.)

The order of appearance within each color block is generally the order of peak bloom. The heading for each species indicates the span of months in which the plants can be found in bloom in the geographical area shown on the map. In the center of that area, the greatest number of plants of a given species will be in bloom or be most noticeable in about the middle of the period shown. There is much overlapping of blooming periods; Bindweed, for example, blooms from May to August, Culver's Root from June to September, but in the same area both will be at their peak about the same time in late July.

The flowers and plants illustrated in the Roadside section are only a few of those you will see along the road. They were chosen because they are colorful, easily seen and recognized, and/or of unusual interest. Most of the photographs were taken from the road or on the shoulder, the view you would have when you pass by. Of the two or more photographs for each plant, one photograph shows the general habitat or growth habit, and thus indicates the relative size or scale to aid you in distinguishing that plant from the surrounding vegetation. A second picture shows the flower as you would see it when you look more closely, and for some plants, there are additional photographs of unusual or interesting features.

A short concluding section of the book illustrates a few of the more showy and familiar flowers that you will find at various seasons if you venture down a path off the road, a brief introduction to some of those that prefer less open or accessible locations.

Throughout the text, references to plants that are described elsewhere in the book are printed in SMALL CAPITALS; you may find them by consulting the index.

Whether you wander far or near, I hope this book will introduce a new and pleasurable aspect to your journey.

Acknowledgments

THANKS ARE due to many people who aided in this compilation. Dr. Hugh H. Iltis, Professor of Botany, University of Wisconsin-Madison, Theodore S. Cochrane and staff members of the University of Wisconsin Herbarium, and Dr. Virginia Kline of the University of Wisconsin Arboretum all assisted in verifying species identifications and references. Dr. James Hall Zimmerman generously allowed me to use a photograph from his collection. Elizabeth Steinberg of the University of Wisconsin Press was an especially patient, helpful, and encouraging editor.

And finally, thanks are due to the one who made this book possible— my husband, Jim, who did the driving, stopped the car on demand, helped lug camera equipment, stood by as we waited for the sun to come out or the rain to cease, and kept his eye on the road and traffic while I recorded the colorful landscape.

Madison, Wisconsin
April 1984

Roadside Plants and Flowers

White Trillium—_Trillium grandiflorum_
White Nodding Trillium—_T. flexipes_

A pristine white flower that borders roadsides and carpets rich woods in an unforgettable array in spring, White Trillium is aptly named _grandiflorum_ ("large-flowered"). It is a handsome early wildflower that may grow up to 18 inches tall with the 2–4-inch blossom held on a flower stalk above three broad leaves. _Trillium_ ("threes") is also a good designation, for all parts are in threes—three white petals, three green sepals, three leaves, six stamens, and three stigmas. This is a relatively long-lasting spring flower, unlike most other early arrivals; it may bloom for two to four weeks, often turning pink as it ages, and the distinctive leaves persist until late summer. Despite the fact that there may appear to be "trillions of trillies," it is a protected and threatened plant that should not be picked. This North American native reversed the usual pattern of plant exchange and was one of the first to make the trip back to the Old World to be cultivated in English gardens.

There are several other equally attractive but less spectacular species of Trilliums in our area that you must seek out, as they very seldom grow close to the road. The White Nodding Trillium (_T. flexipes_) is smaller, and the flower hangs face down. Of the maroon-colored species, the Wake Robin (_T. erectum_) is the most common, so-called because it presumably greets the robins as they migrate north.

Do not pick.

2

1 White Trillium (*Trillium grandiflorum*)
2 White Trillium (*T. grandiflorum*)
3 White Trillium (*T. grandiflorum*): mature pink stage
4 White Nodding Trillium (*T. flexipes*)

Mayapple (Umbrella-leaf, Wild Mandrake, Wild Lemon)— *Podophyllum peltatum*

Mayapples seem to thrust up through the ground in dense patches almost overnight in early spring, forming handsome stands above bare ground and under near-leafless trees. The pointed stalks quickly unfold umbrella-fashion, bearing one or two lobed leaves as much as a foot across. Although Mayapples prefer open woods, where they grow from underground rhizomes, you will occasionally see a near-perfect circle growing on an open hillside or meadow, like a dark green disc left abandoned in the field.

The single, waxy flower that appears in May can be seen only at close range, for it nods beneath its parasol of leaves. The 2-inch blossom grows on a short stem from the angle of two leaf stalks, and only the plants with two leaves will flower. In midsummer the fruit appears, a lemon-colored berry, which accounts for another of the plant's common names, Wild Lemon. The fruit has a distinctive taste (which appeals to some few) and can be made into an unusual jelly, but all other parts of the plant are more or less poisonous. At one time the roots were made into a powerful drug, albeit highly toxic if taken in quantity, and their resemblance to the roots of the unrelated Old World Mandrake gave it another common name, Wild Mandrake.

Do not pick.

Pussytoes (Cat's Foot, Ladies' Tobacco)—*Antennaria fallax*

So-called Pussytoes, of which there are numerous species and variants, appear in late April or May, as a gray-white sprinkling of low-growing plants on dry soil and barren areas along the road. They stand erect on 4–6-inch woolly stems, topped with fuzzy clusters of blossoms in which some people see a resemblance to kittens' paws, hence the common name. (The reason for another common term, Ladies' Tobacco, remains a mystery.) Male and female flowers are borne on separate plants, but it is difficult to distinguish between them; presumably this matters only to the individual plants.

Although not particularly pretty, Pussytoes are noticeable because they come early when there is little else in competition, and often form large colonies. The dried flower heads, country folk used to think, perhaps erroneously, would discourage moths when placed in woollen clothing. Some Indians made a chewing gum from the stalks, but there were undoubtedly better sources for that, too.

1 Mayapple (*Podophyllum peltatum*)
2 Mayapple (*P. peltatum*)
3 Mayapple fruit
4 Pussytoes (*Antennaria fallax*)
5 Pussytoes (*A. fallax*)

False Solomon's Seal (Solomon's Plume, False Spikenard)—*Smilacina racemosa*
Solomon's Seal—*Polygonatum biflorum*

Solomon's Seal—true or False—stands out along the roadside, not so much for its flowering as for its knee-high, graceful growth. The single unbranched and arching stems often abound in beds, and the two plants are frequently found together.

False Solomon's Seal is native to North America and is named for its similarity to its look-alike, more widespread neighbor. Both grow from spreading rootstalks, with leaves that zigzag up a stout stem. They are easily told apart, however; a cluster of starry white flowers grows on the end of the stem of False Solomon's Seal, and in late summer, bright red berries appear. The greenish-white blossoms of Solomon's Seal are bell-like and dangle beneath the stalk from the leaf axils, usually in pairs (*biflorum* means "two-flowered," but there may be one or even three or more blossoms). The berries are a deep blue-black. The leaves and berries persist into late fall, forming golden curves along the highway.

The name Solomon's Seal probably comes from the resemblance of the scar on the root stalk to that of a seal impressed on wax, but it may have come about because the crushed root stalk was considered healing or "sealing" on a wound.

6

1 False Solomon's Seal (*Smilacina racemosa*)
2 False Solomon's Seal (*S. racemosa*)
3 False Solomon's Seal berries
4 Solomon's Seal (*Polygonatum biflorum*)
5 Solomon's Seal fall berries

Queen Anne's Lace (Wild Carrot)—*Daucus carota*

Queen Anne's Lace, which grows all over the world and thrives almost everywhere except in the far northern part of our area or in dense shade, is a delight to many for its decorative, geometric design but a plague for farmers. It often grows in waves along the roadside and across fields and waste places.

The blossom is a lacy, flat-topped 2–5-inch cluster of tiny white flowers, each on a slender stem radiating from the center, and often has a single dark purple floret in the center. The common name supposedly comes from the flower's resemblance to the lace of Queen Anne's headdress, and the tiny purple floret presumably represents a drop of blood where she pricked her finger while making the lace. Many of the old flower clusters fold up, cuplike, resembling small birds' nests.

This biennial plant is also known as Wild Carrot. It is the ancestor of our garden carrot, and the first-year taproot is edible, in moderation, when boiled. Queen Anne's Lace makes a nice addition to a summer bouquet, and because of its rank and sometimes troublesome growth, it can be picked freely. If you add a few drops of food dye to the water, you will have colorful "lace."

1   Queen Anne's Lace (*Daucus carota*)
2   Queen Anne's Lace (*D. carota*)
3   Queen Anne's Lace: "bird's nest"
    flower heads

Cow Parsnip (Masterwort)—*Heracleum lanatum*
Angelica—*Angelica atropurpurea*
Water Hemlock (Cowbane)—*Cicuta maculata*

In addition to QUEEN ANNE'S LACE, which is surely the prettiest wild member of the Parsley family, you will find many other related plants with flat white flower clusters from late spring on. It is difficult to distinguish between them without a technical guide and close examination, and many are poisonous. In fact, one common one—Poison Hemlock (*Conium maculatum*)—is reputed to be the base of the deadly brew that was given Socrates. Ironically, the family also includes such valuable produce as celery, carrot, parsnip, and dill. The family name, Umbelliferae, refers to the flowering umbels, meaning that the blossom clusters are on the tips of stems that radiate like the ribs of an open umbrella.

The many species go by very confusing names: Hemlock-Parsley, Hemlock-Parsnip, Water Hemlock, Water Parsley, Hedge Parsley, Fool's Parsley. Three very common ones, however, are relatively easy to recognize. Cow Parsnip, conspicuous by its size, is a giant plant that grows up to 10 feet tall in moist areas along the road. The enormous maplelike leaves may be as much as 1 foot across, the flower cluster 8 inches, and the thick, woolly, hollow stem 2 inches in diameter. A very similar colossus is Angelica, which is ranker and has a smooth, more purple stem. Neither of these is poisonous, and some parts are edible, but eating them is not advisable because of their resemblance to their toxic relatives. Water Hemlock is one of these, a plant dangerously poisonous to man and animal. This, too, has purple streaks on the stem, but it does not grow as tall as Cow Parsnip and Angelica, and the flower cluster looks like a looser version of Queen Anne's Lace. The leaves are one clue to the various species. The leaves of Queen Anne's Lace (and Poison Hemlock, Fool's Parsley, and Hemlock-Parsley) are finely divided and fernlike; those of the others are coarser, toothed, and/or compound. In all, a very curious group of plants that is not likely to be overlooked.

1 Cow Parsnip (*Heracleum lanatum*)
2 Cow Parsnip (*H. lanatum*)
3 Angelica (*Angelica atropurpurea*)
4 Water Hemlock (*Cicuta maculata*)

Yarrow (Milfoil, Nosebleed Plant)—*Achillea millefolium*

Yarrow blooms about the same time and in many of the same places as QUEEN ANNE'S LACE; the flat-topped flower cluster might be mistaken for it at a distance by a casual observer. However, it is a stiffer plant, and the 2–2½-inch flower head is more densely packed and often more grayish in color. Occasionally a pinkish bloom will be found as well. The fernlike leaves are stalkless; *millefolium* means "thousand-leaved."

Both the alien species (*A. millefolium*) and a native species (*A. lanulosa*) are widespread and so similar that it is very difficult to tell them apart. The genus name comes from the belief that during the Trojan War Achilles found the plant useful for staunching the bleeding of wounds. Others have had faith that chewing the leaves, which are aromatic when crushed and slightly acid, would cure toothache.

Yarrow can be dried for winter bouquets, and the small flower heads are often sprayed green and used to represent trees in architectural scale models.

Meadowrue—*Thalictrum dasycarpum*
Early Meadowrue—*T. dioicum*

It is not difficult to recognize Meadowrue, with its airy, graceful cluster of minute flowers; but determining the species is more difficult. The midseason Tall Meadowrue (*T. polygamum*), also known as King of the Meadow, is bound to command attention along the road, for it often grows to 7 feet, head and shoulders above competing vegetation, and prefers open, moist locations where the crowns of the feathery, dangling flowers dance in the wind.

Meadowrues as a whole have some oddities. The color of the flowers, which have no petals, is greenish-white, yellowish, or mauve, according to the color of the many stamens. Some species have only stamens or pistils in each flower on different plants; others have both in the same flower. In some the stamens dangle like little tassels; in others they stand erect. In any case, the three-lobed leaves, rather resembling those of RUE ANEMONE or WILD COLUMBINE, add to the handsome and distinctive appearance of this plant.

12

1 Yarrow (*Achillea millefolium*)
2 Yarrow (*A. millefolium*)
3 Meadowrue (*Thalictrum dasycarpum*)
4 Early Meadowrue (*T. dioicum*)

13

Ox-eye Daisy (Field Daisy, Marguerite)—*Chrysanthemum leucanthemum*
Mayweed (Stinking Daisy, Dog Fennel, Stinking Chamomile)—*Anthemis cotula*

The familiar and beloved Ox-eye Daisy is a European immigrant that has made itself very much at home here. It comes early and stays late; in England they say that spring has not arrived until you can stand amidst twelve daisies. The sweep of white along a road at its blooming peak may, in fact, resemble snowy drifts of a belated blizzard. It is a favorite plant of artists, photographers, and anxious lovers who play "He loves me, he loves me not" while pulling off the variable number of "petals." These are actually not petals but ray flowers—that is, individual flowers resembling petals. The yellow center is the sun of this "day's eye," or daisy, and consists of numerous tiny disk flowers. Abundant and persistent, it can be picked liberally, and is long-lasting. Farmers are not as enamored with it as poets and others are, for it pervades pastures, and the milk from cattle who graze on it will have an unpleasant taste.

A first quick glance at a mass of similar shorter 1-inch white flowers crowding the road edge may lead you to think that they are stunted daisies, but closer inspection will reveal that, quite apart from the size, Mayweed has a very different, fernlike leaf and a disagreeable odor. (If you make too close an inspection, you may find that the bruised leaves may raise blisters as well.) Confusion about this flower is compounded, for you might be seeing the look-alike Scentless Chamomile (*Matricaria maritima*), or another, the so-called Wild Chamomile (*M. chamomilla*). Your nose will know, for one has no odor and the other has a pineapple-like scent. But it is more likely that you have found the rampant Mayweed. In keeping with its rather unattractive qualities, it thrives where manure has been dumped and abounds in barnyards. Animals, even insects, are repelled by it. Strangely enough, a tea brewed from Mayweed was once believed to cure hysteria; it seems far more likely that the hysteria was brought on by the very thought of such a potion. The Chamomiles were used for a palatable tea, and it is to be hoped that the colonists were astute at distinguishing between them.

1 Ox-eye Daisy (*Chrysanthemum leucanthemum*)
2 Ox-eye Daisy (*C. leucanthemum*)
3 Mayweed (*Anthemis cotula*)
4 Mayweed (*A. cotula*)

15

Wild Cucumber (Balsam Apple)—*Echinocystis lobata*

For a brief period in early summer, the ribbons of showy white flowers of Wild Cucumber festoon hedges, fence rows, and moist thickets. The male flowers stand erect on the long 8–12-foot stems draped over any available support. The female flowers hang below in the leaf axils. The large, attractive leaves are five-pointed and maplelike.

Pretty as Wild Cucumber is in flower, it is even more interesting later when the 2-inch spiny seed pods are visible. These become papery as they mature, pop open, and eject four 1-inch seeds.

The scientific name comes from the Greek, meaning "spiny bladder," referring to the fruit. Some years this plant is particularly abundant and spectacular.

Virgin's Bower (Old Man's Beard)—*Clematis virginiana*

Virgin's Bower, often flowering at the same time and in the same area as WILD CUCUMBER, is also draped over fence rows and shrubs; with its showy white blossoms it may, at first glance, be confused with its neighbor. And this plant, too, is distinctive after its brief blossoming, for its seeds develop soft, feathery plumes, the "old man's beard" of the other common name.

The flowers are in starry clusters arising from the axils of three-part leaflets, with male and female flowers on separate plants. The billows of silvery tails persist until late fall.

1   Wild Cucumber (*Echinocystis lobata*)
2   Wild Cucumber (*E. lobata*)
3   Wild Cucumber seed pods
4   Virgin's Bower (*Clematis virginiana*)
5   Virgin's Bower (*C. virginiana*)
6   Virgin's Bower seedheads

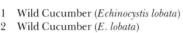

Field Bindweed (Wild Morning Glory, Creeping Jenny, Hellweed)—
Convolvulus arvensis
Hedge Bindweed—*C. sepium*

The pretty little white or pinkish flowers of the Field Bindweed, often growing from a low mat on the roadside, conceal an outlaw from Europe that is heartily disliked for its persistence in cultivated areas. The name *Convolvulus*, from the Latin *convolvere*, "to entwine," accurately describes its growing habit of twisting clockwise about any support or host plant.

The Hedge Bindweed is also readily seen along the road; this species has a larger 2–3-inch flower, usually tinged with pink, and puts on a handsome display during the morning hours, closing up later in the day.

Bindweeds—of which there are many species, some native to North America—are in the Morning Glory family. One wild relative called Man-of-the-Earth (*Ipomoea pandurata*) has 3-inch white flowers, but is more notable for the huge root it forms, a tuber that may weigh as much as 20 pounds.

JUNE—SEPTEMBER
Culver's Root (Culver's Physic)—*Veronicastrum virginicum*

The graceful, tapered blossom spires towering over the surrounding vegetation in moist ditches, thickets, and meadows in midsummer belong to plants with the strange name Culver's Root. The root of the plant is a powerful emetic and cathartic, and possibly a man named Culver, doctor or not, dispensed it freely. In any case, the Indians knew about it first.

The erect stems, encircled with a whorl of three to seven leaves, grow up to 7 feet tall. The tiny flowers, with a faint bluish tinge, gradually open up along the length of the terminal spike, and the projecting style and stamens from each little flower appear feathery.

1 Field Bindweed (*Convolvulus arvensis*)
2 Field Bindweed (*C. arvensis*)
3 Hedge Bindweed (*C. sepium*)
4 Culver's Root (*Veronicastrum virginicum*)
5 Culver's Root (*V. virginicum*)

Boneset (Thoroughwort)—*Eupatorium perfoliatum*
White Snakeroot—*E. rugosum*

Boneset is not the most handsome of the many tall, late-summer-flowering plants, but it is certainly among the most curious because of the old belief that the leaves, wrapped in bandages around broken bones, would help them mend, and that tea made from dried leaves and flower heads would cure "break bone," or dengue fever. Perhaps faith in the healing power rather than any medicinal value accounts for its questionable efficacy.

There are numerous species of *Eupatorium*, but this one is distinctive because the stems appear to grow right through the rather hairy, wrinkled leaves. This characteristic also accounts for another name, Thoroughwort ("through-the-leaves").

A close relative, White Snakeroot, looks similar at first glance, but the flower head is daintier and the leaves have stalks; the plant prefers a more shaded area. Attractive though White Snakeroot may be, it is poisonous, and cattle grazing on it transmit what is known as "milk sickness." This is considered to be the illness that caused the death of Abraham Lincoln's mother, Nancy.

Pearly Everlasting—*Anaphalis margaritacea*
Sweet Everlasting (Catfoot)—*Gnaphalium obtusifolium*

At its peak in August, Pearly Everlasting, which appears in dry open areas and on the shoulders of the road, often forms seemingly endless patches in the more northern part of our area. It is most notable for its "everlasting" quality; it can be picked, hung up to dry, and then added to winter bouquets. The blossom is a flat cluster of yellow flowers enclosed by petallike papery white bracts; male and female flowers are usually on separate plants. Thoreau called this "the artificial flower of the September pasture." The leaves, which have a slight, pleasant odor, are long, gray-green on top, and a cottony white underneath. Indians believed that smoke from the burning leaves would relieve faintness.

A less showy relative, Sweet Everlasting, is more fragrant and more solitary. The tight little flower heads look like buds always on the verge of opening.

1 Boneset (*Eupatorium perfoliatum*)
2 Boneset (*E. perfoliatum*)
3 White Snakeroot (*E. rugosum*)
4 Pearly Everlasting (*Anaphalis margaritacea*)
5 Pearly Everlasting (*A. margaritacea*)
6 Sweet Everlasting (*Gnaphalium obtusifolium*)

21

Marsh Marigold (Cowslip)—*Caltha palustris*

Marsh Marigolds are an early herald of spring; their bright yellow 1–1½-inch blossoms seem to be sunlit even on a cloudy day in April or May. The handsome clumps are easily spotted along the road in wet ditches, meadows, or marshes, for little else blooms in such areas at this time. "The flower that opens the swamps" is how the Indians referred to it. The blossoms, up to 1½ inches across, have glossy, petallike sepals above a mound of kidney-shaped leaves on branched, hollow stems. They resemble buttercups, and are in the same family; the name "marigold," something of a misnomer, comes from the use of the flower in church festivals honoring the Virgin Mary in the Middle Ages. The leaves and stems of the Marsh Marigold have been used as a pot herb, and the buds are sometimes pickled.

Watch for this golden show early, for it is short-lived and the plants disappear by summer.

Do not pick.

Tall Buttercup (Meadow Buttercup)—*Ranunculus acris*
Swamp Buttercup (Marsh Buttercup)—*R. septentrionalis*

The Tall or Meadow Buttercup, which gives a yellow sheen to fields and meadows and glistens along roadsides, is beloved of poets and a favorite of children, who like to hold a blossom under one's chin and ask, "Do you like butter?" (The resulting reflection on the skin may, indeed, indicate too much fondness for butter or other fats.) The name "buttercup" comes from the belief that the flower gave yellow color to butter, but this is fancy, not fact, for grazing cattle usually avoid it. The epithet *acris* refers to its acrid taste. Some of the more than twenty other common species of Buttercups are more or less poisonous, and all give milk an unpalatable flavor.

The shiny petals of the 1-inch flowers appear to be varnished and make attractive additions to a bouquet, although they may shatter readily if picked when mature. The common Tall Buttercup is an introduced species, but the very similar Swamp Buttercup is a North American native. This shorter species blooms earlier, has larger flowers, and is found in more moist areas and woodlands.

1 Marsh Marigold (*Caltha palustris*)
2 Marsh Marigold (*C. palustris*)
3 Tall Buttercup (*Ranunculus acris*)
4 Tall Buttercup (*R. acris*)
5 Swamp Buttercup (*R. septentrionalis*)

23

Winter Cress—*Barbarea vulgaris*

About the same time that dandelions are blooming profusely, several other hardy, aggressive "weeds" turn roadsides, meadows, and waste places a bright yellow. They may so blanket a field as to appear planted, and in some cases, they were. They are members of the Mustard family, and various species of two genera go by such common names as Winter Cress, Yellow Rocket, Yellow Cress, and Black, Field, and Chinese Mustard. They all have flowers with four petals, bunched on the ends of 1–3-foot stems, and produce elongated seed pods. Winter Cress (*Barbarea vulgaris*) appears first, but beyond that, it takes close examination of the leaves and seed pods to distinguish between the species. The flowers are not particularly attractive, but their rank abundance makes the plants very conspicuous.

The seeds of Black Mustard (*Brassica nigra*) are used in the preparation of the condiment mustard, and the plant is cultivated for this purpose, but the seeds of some others are also edible. The rampant spread of these plants, most of which were introduced into North America, is due primarily to the scattering of their numerous minute seeds, some of which have been known to sprout after many years of dormancy.

Leafy Spurge—*Euphorbia esula*
Flowering Spurge—*E. corollata*

Fields with a soft green-gold glow or a roadside that is gilt-edged signals the presence of Leafy Spurge or its look-alike relative, Cypress Spurge (*E. cyparissias*). Leafy Spurge is something of a scourge, for, once established, it is difficult to eradicate and is rated as a "noxious pest" in some areas. Nevertheless, it is worth a close look because of its odd flower arrangement. The blossoms are in a loose umbel; two kidney-shaped flower-leaves on a short stem are topped by two yellow-green petallike bracts around the curious tiny flowers.

There are many quite dissimilar Spurges. The family includes the poinsettia, for example, and the rubber tree. Most Spurges have a milky juice or sap which may be somewhat poisonous, and share the characteristic of lacking flower petals; all have separate male and female flowers. Flowering Spurge is one common relative bearing little resemblance to Leafy Spurge; it thrives in dry, rocky roadsides. The small white flowers of this plant are modest and unpretentious alone, but the plants en masse make an attractive, airy stand.

1 Winter Cress (*Barbarea vulgaris*)
2 Winter Cress (*B. vulgaris*)
3 Leafy Spurge (*Euphorbia esula*)
4 Leafy Spurge (*E. esula*)
5 Flowering Spurge (*E. corollata*)
6 Flowering Spurge (*E. corollata*)

Black-eyed Susan (Brown-eyed Susan)—*Rudbeckia hirta*

Black-eyed Susan, abundant and long-blooming, dots roadsides and meadows from early summer to frost. The leaves and stems are rough and hairy, the petals (ray flowers) a clear, bright yellow, and the center (composed of numerous small disk flowers) chocolate-colored. This native of the prairie states has moved eastward and is now the state flower of Maryland. It is long-lasting as a cut flower and makes a glowing bouquet. Who "Susan" was remains a mystery.

Mullein (Flannel Leaf, Velvet Leaf, Candlewick)—*Verbascum thapsus*

Long after flowering, the stout stalks of Mullein stand stiffly upright, towering sentinels over dry fields and gravelly road shoulders. The blossoms are not very showy because only a few flowers open at a time, at rather random intervals in the tightly packed cluster at the top of the stalk. The plant is, however, handsome and interesting, and widespread both here and in its native Europe.

Mullein is a biennial. The first year a rosette of soft gray-green woolly leaves appears; these persist and stay green during the winter, protected from snow and cold by velvety hairs. The second year a 3–7-foot flowering stalk thrusts upward, occasionally branched like candelabra. The plant has a deep tap root which enables it to endure hot sun and dry weather, but it is not a nuisance weed, for it cannot establish itself in cultivated areas and seeks room to stand apart from competitors. It has had many uses in the past: the dry stalks, which readily soak up oil or tallow, made flaming Roman torches; the soft leaves warded off the cold as lining for footgear of Indians and colonists; numerous medicinal qualities (including a cure for leprosy) have been attributed to it; and superstition credited it with the ability to ward off evil.

Wild Parsnip—*Pastinaca sativa*

A number of tall, rather weedy plants with flat-topped yellow flower clusters are common and widespread in midsummer. Although they are different genera in the Parsley family, they appear deceptively alike, varying primarily in size and shape of leaves and details of stem. The flowers, in an umbel, look somewhat like yellow versions of QUEEN ANNE'S LACE or COW PARSNIP.

The tallest one, Wild Parsnip, has a coarse, hollow, fluted stalk, often branched. Actually it is a garden parsnip brought over from the Old World and now gone wild, an escapee from cultivation. It is a biennial, and by the time you see it in flower, in its second year, all parts of it are poisonous, and the leaves and stalk can cause a severe rash. Its genus name means "to dig," and the first year the root is edible—if you like parsnips.

1 Black-eyed Susan (*Rudbeckia hirta*)
2 Black-eyed Susan (*R. hirta*)
3 Mullein (*Verbascum* sp.): first-year leaf rosette
4 Mullein (*V. thapsus*)
5 Mullein (*V. thapsus*)
6 Wild Parsnip (*Pastinaca sativa*)

The Clovers—*Trifolium* spp.
Melilotus spp.
Petalostemum purpureum

Almost anyone can recognize the Common White Clover (*Trifolium re-pens*), which grows in lawns, and many of us have searched for a "good luck" four-leafed aberrant of this plant, whose genus name, *Trifolium*, means "three-leaved." Sweet-scented, rosy-hued fields of Red Clover (*T. pratense*), sown for forage and soil enrichment, are an equally familiar sight in the country, with many plants spilling over to brighten roadsides. Even card players know clover leaves, the symbol for the suit of clubs. *Clava*, the Latin word for "club," was the original name for clover, presumably because the leaf resembled the three-knobbed club of Hercules. While *clava* was corrupted to "clover," the word "club" continued to be used for the playing cards.

The pretty, fuzzy little Rabbit-foot Clover (*T. arvense*) likes stony ground and often edges the road with a velvety pinkish-gray bloom, as soft to the touch as rabbit's fur. You may find this growing with the yellow Low Hop Clover (*T. campestre*), which gets its name from the fact that the flower clusters wither and fold down, resembling dried hops.

Two tall and rather straggly bush plants, with little resemblance to the genus *Trifolium*, are called Sweet Clovers (*Melilotus* spp.), one with white and the other with tiny yellow flowers. Once introduced for pasturage, both are widespread on roadsides. Yellow Sweet Clover (*M. officinalis*) is particularly fragrant, and the dried heads can be made into sachets with a pleasant vanillalike odor.

A native so-called clover, the Purple Prairie Clover (*Petalostemum purpureum*), which you may find in dry prairies, looks even less like the familiar clover of lawn and field. The flower head at the end of a wiry stem is cylindrical, with a fringe of rosy petals on a partly bare cone.

The Clovers vary widely in color, range, and shape, but all are of considerable value to man, beast, and insect.

1 Yellow Sweet Clover (*Melilotus officinalis*)
2 White Sweet Clover (*M. alba*)
3 Rabbit-foot Clover (*Trifolium arvense*) and Low Hop Clover (*T. campestre*)
4 Red Clover (*T. pratense*)
5 Purple Prairie Clover (*Petalostemum purpureum*)

Common Evening Primrose—*Oenothera biennis*

The name "primrose" is apt to bring to mind a perennial garden flower that neither resembles nor is related to our wild Evening Primroses. The 1–2-inch flowers of the Common Evening Primrose have four petals, and appear in a crowded cluster along the top of the plant stem, which may be branched. The plant will appear somewhat unkempt at times, for the blossoms open in late afternoon or early evening and are generally closed during the day. But this is a highly variable species and there are several similar species in the genus, so you may well find an exception with flowers that are open most of the day.

The Common Evening Primrose usually has a reddish stem. The long taproot is considered edible, somewhat like a parsnip. It is a biennial, forming a rosette of leaves the first year and sending up one or more 2–6-foot stems the second. The slight lemony fragrance of the flower is particularly attractive to moths.

Birdfoot Trefoil (Hop-o-My-Thumb, Devil's Claw, Five Fingers)—*Lotus corniculatus*

A decorative roadside edging of Birdfoot Trefoil, with its showy yellow pealike flowers, may almost appear to have been planted—and perhaps it was, for it is sometimes used to prevent erosion. More likely it is a naturalized escapee from a pasture. This legume originally came from Europe and reversed the usual pattern of such aliens: it first went wild and then was "rediscovered" and cultivated for forage and soil conservation.

It has been known under more than fifty names, but the common American name comes from the fact that the 1-inch seed pods resemble a bird's foot. The flower color ranges from lemon yellow to deep orange, sometimes tinged with red. The leaves appear to be in three parts (thus "trefoil"), but actually are in five.

1 Common Evening Primrose (*Oenothera biennis*)
2 Evening Primrose (*Oenothera* sp.)
3 Birdfoot Trefoil (*Lotus corniculatus*)
4 Birdfoot Trefoil (*L. corniculatus*)

31

Coreopsis—*Coreopsis lanceolata*
C. palmata

Coreopsis often forms bright yellow colonies along the road in early summer, for it spreads easily. Some species are grown as garden flowers, and you may find a group that has escaped from cultivation. Most have eight toothed rays in the flower head on a long, slender stem, a feature that distinguishes them from the many equally bright yellow SUNFLOWERS which begin to appear about the same time. Coreopsis is also called Tickseed because the little seedlike fruits resemble black ticks and have tiny barbs enabling them to cling to clothing or fur.

Yellow Goatsbeard (Go-to-Bed-at-Noon)—*Tragopogon dubius*

Yellow Goatsbeard is noticeable not so much for its blossom, which is a rather undistinguished single yellow flower head, as for its dandelion-like seedhead, which is a gigantic "blowball" as much as 5 inches across. The head of pale yellow ray flowers at the top of a 1–3-foot stiff stem generally faces the sun, opening in the morning and closing by midday; hence the plant has been called Go-to-Bed-at-Noon. A closely related species, *T. pratensis*, is known also as Meadow Salsify.

The large seedheads are globular. If they are picked when they first appear, and before time, wind, and rain have damaged their structure, they can be sprayed with a clear lacquer or colored paint to make a long-lasting, filmy decoration.

A purple-flowered species *(T. porrifolius)*, called Oyster Plant or Salsify, may occasionally be found. This is an escapee from cultivation brought to America for its fleshy root, which has a faint flavor of oysters.

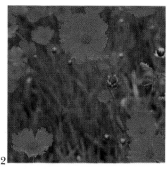

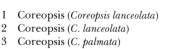

1 Coreopsis (*Coreopsis lanceolata*)
2 Coreopsis (*C. lanceolata*)
3 Coreopsis (*C. palmata*)
4 Yellow Goatsbeard (*Tragopogon dubius*)
  Photo: James Hall Zimmerman
5 Yellow Goatsbeard seedheads
6 Yellow Goatsbeard seedhead

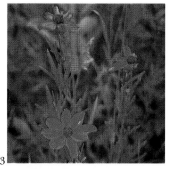

33

Common St.-John's-Wort—*Hypericum perforatum*

St.-John's-Wort is very plentiful in dry, sandy fields and along roadsides in early summer, yet it may not warrant a second glance unless one looks closely at the little yellow flowers. The 1–3-foot branching plants tend to look weedy, for the individual 1-inch blossoms in loose clusters at the top of the stems open briefly and then wither. The petals do not fall off, and the head becomes ragged and untidy. Nevertheless, the individual five-petaled golden flowers are most attractive. The petals are fringed with tiny black dots on the margin, and the numerous erect stamens give the blossom a delicate, starry aspect. Hold a leaf up against the light, and you will find translucent dots.

There are many native species, but Common St.-John's-Wort, most frequently found, is a native of the Old World, and many legends have grown up about the plant. Considered something of a cure-all in the Middle Ages, it was also believed to have the power to ward off evil spirits and was thought to be particularly potent when gathered or burned on St. John's Day, June 24. The dots on the leaves were imagined to be spots where the devil had pricked them; the plant's resistance made the devil fear it thereafter.

Butter-and-Eggs (Yellow Toadflax)—*Linaria vulgaris*

This handsome two-toned butter-yellow and egg-yolk–orange flower, appropriately called Butter-and-Eggs, often grows in large masses close to the road. Despite its fragile appearance, it is a sturdy, erect plant that will bloom fulsomely even after a midseason mowing by highway crews. The flower resembles a small snapdragon, and when it is pinched at the hinge of the two lips, it opens wide; some saw a resemblance to a toad's mouth and termed it Toadflax. The bright orange on the lower lip is a signal for insects seeking nectar and serves to direct them into the spur below.

Once considered an attractive garden flower, it is now so common that its decorative quality is overlooked. In some locales it has been called Ranstead Weed because a man named Ranstead introduced the plants into his garden in the East and they got away.

1 Common St.-John's-Wort (*Hypericum perforatum*)
2 Common St.-John's-Wort (*H. perforatum*)
3 Butter-and-Eggs (*Linaria vulgaris*)
4 Butter-and-Eggs (*L. vulgaris*)

Rough-fruited Cinquefoil—*Potentilla recta*

At a distance, the Rough-fruited Cinquefoil might be mistaken for BUT-TERCUPS, for the erect plants, which make a nice show in dry areas and meadows, have yellow 1-inch blossoms with five petals, and grow 1–3 feet tall. The petals are slightly notched and a rather faded shade of yellow. The name "cinquefoil" means "five-part leaf," and the term is commonly used for all members of the genus *Potentilla*; this is confusing, however, because the number of leaf segments may vary from three to eleven, even within the same species. Then, too, the genus name, "little potent one," refers to the medicinal use of only one species, commonly known as Silverweed (*P. anserina*). The flowers of all Cinquefoils, at least, have five petals, five sepals, and five green bracts (small modified leaves at the base of the flower).

Tansy (Golden Button, Bitter Button)—*Tanacetum vulgare*

Flat clusters of what appear to be bright yellow buttons—flower heads of disk flowers only, with no ray flowers—are the hallmark of Tansy. This plant is so distinctive that it is easily recognized and cannot be mistaken for any other.

It grows up to 5 feet tall, with finely cut, deeply lobed leaves and one or more flower clusters on a single stout stem. An herb of the Old World, it has a strong scent that is a clue to the reason for its centuries-long medicinal usage, as a bitter tea, as a poultice for strains and bruises, and as a substitute for sage, despite its strong aftertaste. Despite its history, it is not to be recommended as either a tea or a seasoning substitute because the oil in the stem and in old leaves is toxic; perhaps its earlier use as a mosquito repellent had some virtue. It does, however, make an attractive, long-lasting bouquet and can be dried for winter floral arrangements.

1 Rough-fruited Cinquefoil (*Potentilla recta*)
2 Rough-fruited Cinquefoil (*P. recta*)
3 Tansy (*Tanacetum vulgare*)
4 Tansy (*T. vulgare*)

37

Prairie Coneflower (Gray-headed Coneflower)—*Ratibida pinnata*
Purple Coneflower—*Echinacea purpurea*

Don't be fooled into thinking that the drooping "petals" (ray flowers) on a tall stand of bright yellow flowers are just those of wilted SUNFLOWERS or BLACK-EYED SUSANS. This plant is a relative of those two flowers, but in dry weather or wet, the rays of the Prairie Coneflower hang down naturally; in botanical terms, they are "reflexed." It has a large dull-colored "button" or cone (of disk flowers) that turns brown, and the head gives off an aniselike odor when crushed.

The name "coneflower" may lead to confusion because it is also used for plants in another genus (*Rudbeckia*). The distinctions are largely technical, but you are most likely to notice the Prairie Coneflower because it grows up to 5 feet tall, has the droopiest appearance, and is most commonly found along the road.

The name is also applied to a flower that, unlike all the others, is not yellow—the Purple Coneflower. This colorful plant with its large magenta blossoms is found wild only in prairies and dry woods in the more southern part of our range—a memorable and uncommon find. *Do not pick.*

Velvet Leaf (Butterprint, Pie Marker)—*Abutilon theophrasti*

This plant, which grows up to 6 feet tall along roadsides, in waste places, and often in cornfields, is more noticeable for its huge heart-shaped velvety leaves than for the small yellow flowers that grow on short stalks from the leaf axils. This is a hot-weather plant; the seed does not sprout until midsummer, at which time it may take off and grow rapidly and fulsomely. It may appear in otherwise well-tended cornfields because its late germination makes it possible to survive the last plowing when the corn is laid by. One of its other common names, Butterprint, comes from the odd circle of little seed pods which resembles the print once used by farm wives to stamp butter; and Pie Marker refers to the pod's resemblance to the crimped edge of pastry.

1 Prairie Coneflower (*Ratibida pinnata*)
2 Prairie Coneflower (*R. pinnata*)
3 Purple Coneflower (*Echinacea purpurea*)
4 Velvet Leaf (*Abutilon theophrasti*)
5 Velvet Leaf pod

Goldenrod—*Solidago* spp.

The Goldenrods are often given wide berth because of the suspicion that they cause hayfever. Although a few persons may be allergic to Goldenrod, it is the wind-blown pollen of another plant, RAGWEED—which flowers at about the same time—that is the real culprit. Very little Goldenrod pollen, which is rather sticky, is air-borne; the plants are pollinated by insects. Most Goldenrods are truly handsome plants with clusters of yellow flower heads in many forms, and they brighten the landscape from late summer through fall in great masses. Because they are such common natives, they are taken for granted in this country, but in England, which has only one native species, they are cultivated as a garden plant. Fishermen also appreciate them because the large round galls on the stems of some contain a larva which makes an excellent, if minute, fish bait. And disregarding an undeserved reputation, Alabama, Kentucky, and Nebraska have named Goldenrod as their state flower.

Although Goldenrod is easily recognized as such, it is very difficult to tell the numerous and variable species apart. One of the major distinctions is the pattern or shape of the cluster of flower heads, which may appear plumelike on outward or downward curved stems, in a tight bunch on an upright stem, or in a flat-topped terminal cluster. One could make a life-long hobby of learning to name the dozens of species which grow in all kinds of terrain in our area.

Giant Ragweed—*Ambrosia trifida*
Common Ragweed—*A. artemisiifolia*

Ragweed, of which there are several species, is the true hayfever villain. Giant Ragweed, with its large, lobed leaves, may grow as much as 15 feet tall; the other common species, *A. artemisiifolia*, Common Ragweed, which has dissected leaves, is shorter (growing up to 5 feet tall). All have long terminal flowering clusters with tiny green flower heads that carry the wretched allergenic yellow pollen. *Ambrosia*, the genus name, meaning "food of the gods," is surely a botanical joke. The plant is so bitter that it spoils the milk of any cow desperate or stupid enough to eat it. It is widespread, as hayfever sufferers know; only in upper Michigan, northern Wisconsin, and parts of Minnesota where it does not grow or is relatively rare, can they find relief. On the plus side, its oil-rich seeds are a valuable source of fall and winter food for birds.

1   Goldenrod (*Solidago* sp.)
2   Goldenrod (*Solidago* sp.)
3   Canada Goldenrod (*S. canadensis*): galls on stem
4   Giant Ragweed (*Ambrosia trifida*)
5   Common Ragweed (*A. artemisiifolia*)

Sunflowers

Common Sunflower—*Helianthus annuus*
Tall Sunflower—*H. giganteus*
Wood Sunflower—*H. strumosus*
Prairie Dock (Elephant Ear)—*Silphium terebinthinaceum*

Those stout, rough plants with bright yellow "petals" (ray flowers) that appear in midsummer are Sunflowers, right? Well, yes and no. Many are true Sunflowers, but others—such as Rosinweeds (*Silphium* spp.), the so-called Tickseed Sunflowers (*Bidens* spp.), and the Ox-eye (*Heliopsis helianthoides*) may be mistaken for Sunflowers.

There are more than twenty species in our area, most of which are native. The Common Sunflower (*Helianthus annuus*), the most familiar, is the state flower of Kansas, and cultivated varieties are grown in gardens and fields, turning their huge, heavy heads to follow the sun during the day. Sunflowers are usually grown for their seeds, useful to man and birds, but one wild Sunflower, inappropriately called Jerusalem Artichoke (*Helianthus tuberosus*), is also cultivated for its edible tuber. Its origin is not Jerusalem; that part of its name comes from the Italian *girasole*, meaning "turning to the sun," and its only relationship to an artichoke is in the faint bland taste of the boiled root.

The Tall Sunflower lives up to its name by sending up a branched stalk that may grow 10 feet tall in roadside ditches. Another widespread species, the Wood Sunflower, may be 4–6 feet tall in dry woods.

Prairie Dock, one of the Rosinweeds and not a true Sunflower, is a tall coarse plant notable for the large basal leaves which give it its other common name, Elephant Ear. Clusters of these huge distinctive leaves can often be seen on plants along the highway before the flowering stalk appears. The blossoms are borne on a slender, almost leafless 6–8-inch stem.

All Sunflowers have ten to twenty-five petallike ray flowers, and the color of the center disk flowers varies. The genus name comes from the Greek *helios*, "sun," and *anthos*, "flower." The Sunflower is a leading contender in the ongoing and long-drawn-out Congressional debate to name a national flower; were it to be selected, the debate would undoubtedly be further complicated by the need to decide the representative native species.

1 Common Sunflower (*Helianthus annuus*): cultivated variety
2 Tall Sunflower (*H. giganteus*)
3 Wood Sunflower (*H. strumosus*)
4 Prairie Dock (*Silphium terebinthinaceum*)
5 Prairie Dock (*S. terebinthinaceum*)

43

Lilies

JUNE–AUGUST
Day Lily—*Hemerocallis fulva*
JUNE–JULY
Wood Lily—*Lilium philadelphicum*
JULY–AUGUST
Turk's Cap—*L. michiganense*
JUNE–AUGUST
Tiger Lily—*L. lancifolium*

Several different orange lilies are roadside or near-roadside inhabitants. The most common, the Day Lily, may blanket the shoulder or roadbank with tawny blossoms and dense light green foliage, often inadvertently spread there by road graders and plows which have dispersed the reproductive tubers. The Day Lily is an alien, a garden escapee that has become widely naturalized. It differs from the true Lilies in that the leaves are basal, long, and pointed, and the flowering stalk is bare. The blossoms are upright and unspotted, and each of the many buds on the stem opens and lasts but a day (the botanical name means "beautiful for a day"). The buds, flowers, and tubers are all edible, and the various parts can be boiled, fried, baked, and pickled, a challenge to a venturesome cook.

The Wood Lily also has an upright blossom, usually only one on a 1–3-foot stalk. It is much less common and more solitary, appearing as a glowing near-scarlet dot of color at the edge of woodlands or in sandy soil. This one is to be admired but not picked.

Two other orange lilies that can be found near the road, one native, Turk's Cap, and one from Asia, Tiger Lily, have nodding, spotted blossoms. Both are spectacular plants, growing to a height of 6 feet or more, with many flowers arching out from a single, tall stem. The petals of these two are sharply bent back. The name Turk's Cap comes from the blossom's supposed resemblance to a sultan's headdress, but Tiger Lily is an inaccurate reference: tigers have stripes, not spots (Tiger Lily was formerly designated *L. tigrinum*, but the species name has been changed to *L. lancifolium*—an example of the way botanists refine nomenclature from time to time). Although very similar in appearance, these two Lilies can be told apart by their leaves, which are in whorls on the stem of the Turk's Cap and alternate on the stem of the Tiger Lily. The latter has distinctive "beads," dark little bulblets in the leaf axils.

Do not pick any but Day Lily.

1 Day Lily (*Hemerocallis fulva*)
2 Day Lily (*H. fulva*)
3 Turk's Cap (*Lilium michiganense*)
4 Turk's Cap (*L. michiganense*)
5 Wood Lily (*L. philadelphicum*)
6 Tiger Lily (*L. lancifolium*)

45

Butterfly Weed (Orange Milkweed, Pleurisy Root)—*Asclepias tuberosa*
Marsh Milkweed (Swamp Milkweed)—*A. incarnata*

A flash of brilliant orange along the road in an open sandy or gravelly area is a sure sign of Butterfly Weed. The clumps or single plants, a foot high or more, are a startling blaze here and there and one of the showiest wayside flowers. This is a native plant of prairies and open places, and is a member of the Milkweed family, but its juice is watery, not milky. The blossoms often attract hordes of butterflies—monarchs are particularly fond of it. The plant has a long tap root which enables it to withstand drought and mowing; it may even bloom a second time. In the past the root was boiled and used to treat pleurisy, which accounts for its less common name, but there is little evidence of any medicinal value. The flower clusters, about 2 inches across, are composed of numerous little flowers with a slight, pleasant fragrance.

You will find Marsh Milkweed in very different terrain—marshes, wet prairies, or streambanks. The flower head, somewhat flatter than that of Butterfly Weed, is a rosy-pink, the leaves are narrow and pointed, and the plant grows to 4 feet or more. It may be found with JOE-PYE-WEED, for which it might be mistaken until one looks closely at the pretty little flowers.

Orange Hawkweed (Devil's Paintbrush)—*Hieracium aurantiacum*
King Devil—*H. florentinum*

A dry roadside dotted with small, 3/4-inch red-orange flowers, interspersed with very similar yellow ones, and often the white of daisies, is a good sign that you are in Hawkweed country. Adjacent open fields, too, may be aglow with the same orange hue. Hawkweed is scorned as a pernicious weed, coarse and hairy, but Orange Hawkweed deserves a closer look: it boasts very pretty flower heads with their numerous fringed ray flowers delicately shaded from yellow in the center to deep orange on the margins. The plant grows 8–24 inches tall from a rosette of leaves, with a single erect unbranched stem; one or more of the flower heads in the tight terminal cluster opens daily, to be replaced by a new blossom the next day.

Several other species of Hawkweed, such as King Devil, have yellow flower heads that resemble tall dandelions. Most are aliens. The name "hawkweed" comes from the Old World belief that hawks sharpened their eyesight by eating the blossoms, a highly fanciful supposition.

1 Butterfly Weed (*Asclepias tuberosa*)
2 Butterfly Weed (*A. tuberosa*)
3 Marsh Milkweed (*A. incarnata*)
4 Orange Hawkweed (*Hieracium aurantiacum*)
5 Orange Hawkweed (*H. aurantiacum*)
6 King Devil (*H. florentinum*)

Wild Columbine (Rock Bells)—*Aquilegia canadensis*

You will find the two-toned scarlet and yellow blossoms of Wild Columbine dangling airily along sloping rock cuts beside the road and at the edge of rocky woods in early summer. Although it self-sows freely, it is no great colonizer, and each plant seems to seek elbow room to stand well apart from its neighbors. Despite its apparent fragility, it grows with perennial persistence from a deep rootstalk, well adapted to withstand drought.

The name "columbine" comes from the Latin *columba*, meaning "dove," a reference to a fanciful resemblance of the five long-spurred petals to a ring of doves. The literary namesake, Columbine, is characterized as "saucy and adroit," perhaps a more fitting description for both of them.

The delicate, scalloped foliage is as attractive as the blossoms. The nodding flowers, with their backward- or upward-pointing tubes, attract many long-tongued insects and hummingbirds. These spurs apparently inspired the generic name, derived from the Latin *aquila*, meaning "eagle," referring to a far-fetched likeness to an eagle's talons. The "beaked" seed pods, which open along one side when ripe, carry out the avian allusion.

This Columbine is a widespread native eastern species; many others are found in the West, and one is the state flower of Colorado. A European import, *A. vulgaris*, with blue, pink, and violet flowers having shorter spurs, is cultivated, and occasionally escapes to grow wild.

Indian Paintbrush (Painted Cup)—*Castilleja coccinea*

This plant is well named, for the tip ends appear to have been dipped in a pot of red paint. There is a legend that says the plant sprang up where an Indian discarded his brushes after painting a sunset. The blossom color comes from the red-tipped bracts, which hide the tiny real flowers.

You will see this plant growing in damp, sandy soil of open meadows and along the edge of woods, bright red spots dotted through the grass upon which its roots are said to be parasitic. The plants grow up to 2 feet tall.

There are other western species called Painted Cup, but *C. coccinea* is the common one (and the only red-flowered one) of the Great Lakes area.

Do not pick.

48

1   Wild Columbine (*Aquilegia canadensis*)
2   Wild Columbine (*A. canadensis*)
3   Indian Paintbrush (*Castilleja coccinea*)
4   Indian Paintbrush (*C. coccinea*)

Prairie Smoke (Long-plumed Avens, Grandpa's Whiskers)—*Geum triflorum*

If you are fortunate enough to catch a glimpse of a reddish cast over a dry field near the road in late spring, you will do well to stop for a look at a most unusual plant, aptly named Prairie Smoke. The range of this species is limited, so it is rather special, although there are other more widespread and less interesting Avens in the *Geum* genus.

The flower is a tight little nodding crimson globe; there are usually three flowers on a short, 6–15-inch stem, with small fernlike lower leaves. The real show starts when the flower develops into a fruit, to trail soft 2-inch mauve plumes in the wind, like a delicate puff of smoke. The plants often form clumps in sunny areas, and tend to crowd out meadow grasses as they spread.

Do not pick.

Wild Rose—*Rosa* sp.

The country cousins of the familiar cultivated roses grow abundantly along roadsides and fence rows in early summer. Wild Roses have but five petals, and the colors range from near-white to a deep rose, with single blossoms or small clusters. There are numerous species, distinguished primarily by the number and kind of thorns—some with sharp spines, some with mere prickles, and others nearly thornless—and by the number of leaflets, from three to nine. Some grow tall on long canes, and others are low shrubs.

The various common names given to them—Prairie Rose, Swamp Rose, Pasture or Meadow Rose, Prickly Rose, and so on—often do not refer to the same species, and inasmuch as the species hybridize readily, it is often difficult to tell which one you have found. It is enough, perhaps, to enjoy their wild beauty and their fragrance.

The fruit of the rose, known as a "hip," is a glossy round red globe that is very noticeable by late summer. This is a favored fruit of wild birds. It is rich in vitamin C and is sometimes made into jelly.

1   Prairie Smoke (*Geum triflorum*)
2   Prairie Smoke (*G. triflorum*)
3   Wild Rose (*Rosa* sp.)
4   Wild Rose (*Rosa* sp.)
5   Wild Rose hips

51

JUNE–AUGUST
Common Milkweed—*Asclepias syriaca*
JUNE–SEPTEMBER
Whorled Milkweed—*A. verticillata*

The Common Milkweed is easily recognized and widespread. It is a tall, robust plant with large rubbery leaves and exudes a milky, sticky juice when cut or bruised. Although it is not particularly notable for its beauty, it has some uncommon features which might make it of interest. The small, fragrant mauve flowers grow in tennis-ball–sized clusters which usually droop from the axils of the upper leaves. Close examination of the miniature individual flowers will reveal an unusual structure of five down-pointed petals below a crown of five stamens fused to the enlarged stigma and each bearing a hood-shaped appendage containing an incurved horn. The rich nectar within the hoods attracts insects, but only one or two of the plant's distinctive warty pods develop from the clusters of many flowers. The flower heads, picked when still in tight buds, can be boiled and buttered for a savory side dish similar to broccoli.

The Common Milkweed also serves as the chief food of the larvae of monarch butterflies, and for good reason. The leaves contain a substance which makes the larva and adult butterfly toxic to birds. (In turn, another butterfly, the viceroy, takes on a close resemblance to the beautiful monarch, in an effort to warn off assailants, although it does not have the same protective bitterness itself.)

In late summer, the pods split open along one side, revealing precisely packed little seeds with long silky hairs which open like parachutes as the seeds are dispersed by the wind. This "silk" has been used to stuff pillows and was substituted for kapok in life preservers during World War I. The dried open pods make an interesting addition to a winter arrangement.

Another Milkweed, *A. verticillata*, is not as easily recognized as such, although it, too, has a milky juice and forms small pods. The Whorled Milkweed, which often borders roads en masse and invades meadows, has white blossoms on a shorter, unbranched stem and narrow leaves in whorls of three to six about the stem. Two other species of Milkweed are the BUTTERFLY WEED and MARSH MILKWEED.

1   Common Milkweed (*Asclepias syriaca*)
2   Common Milkweed (*A. syriaca*)
3   Common Milkweed silk
4   Whorled Milkweed (*A. verticillata*)
5   Whorled Milkweed silk

53

Bouncing Bet (Soapwort, Lady-by-the-Gate, Old Maid's Pink)—
Saponaria officinalis

Bouncing Bet pops up in wastelands, along highways, and particularly, in or near gravelly railroad beds. Slightly disheveled but sturdy and profuse, Bouncing Bet is not much good for bouquets but has other virtues.

Although it is often found in large colonies, formed by underground spreading roots, it stays well out of the way of farmers and gardeners. The colonists brought it from England, perhaps because of its usefulness as a substitute for soap. The leaves and stems make a soapy lather when crushed, and these suds were used for fine silks and woollens, glass and china, in place of the harsh homemade lye soap. This accounts for one of its other common names, Soapwort ("wort" meaning "plant"), and "Bouncing Bet" is also an old-fashioned colloquialism for "washerwoman."

The phloxlike flower is slightly fragrant, and the plants grow 1–3 feet tall. You may occasionally see a rosier patch of double-petaled blooms, but the flowers are usually a pale pink or near-white. The plant is a member of the Pink family, and once you've met "Bet" you'll not forget her.

Physostegia (Obedient Plant, False Dragonhead)—*Physostegia virginiana*

A flower that stays in whatever position it is placed when the stalk is bent is worth noting if for no other reason than this odd trait. This plant is sometimes called Obedient Plant; its other common name, False Dragonhead, seems to have little relevance, and the true name, Physostegia, is a bit of a tongue-twister.

It is a rather unprepossessing plant that grows in moist ditches and thickets. The pale rose or lavender blossoms are lipped, somewhat in the manner of snapdragons, and grow in 4–8-inch spikes from the axils of willowlike, toothed leaves or at the top of the stem. Only a few flowers open at a time, projecting at a stiff angle to the tight spike. The square stem and opposite leaves identify it as a member of the Mint family. Both the common pink-flowered form and a white-flowered form are sometimes cultivated in the garden.

1 Bouncing Bet (*Saponaria officinalis*)
2 Bouncing Bet (*S. officinalis*)
3 Physostegia (*Physostegia virginiana*)
4 Physostegia (*P. virginiana*)

Steeplebush (Hardhack)—*Spiraea tomentosa*
Meadowsweet (Quaker Lady)—*S. alba*

Foamy, tapered flower clusters appear on two very similar shrubs about the same time and from the road are a bit difficult to tell apart. Of the two, the blossoms of Steeplebush are a deeper pink and form a more conical spire. Steeplebush also has leaves that are a woolly brown underneath. The tough, woody stem gives it its other name, Hardhack, for it was difficult to cut back when it was growing in a pasture. The tiny florets in the "steeple" open from the top down, in reverse of the order of many other plants, and this leaves a faded brownish tip as the blossoming progresses.

Meadowsweet blossoms are whiter, with a slight pinkish cast from the numerous stamens, and are in a looser cluster. The leaves are hairless. At one time they were scattered on bare floors during banquets to give the air a sweet fragrance.

Both plants in blossom add a grace note to roadsides and meadows, often in concert with such other sunlovers as QUEEN ANNE'S LACE and MILKWEED.

Spreading Dogbane—*Apocynum androsaemifolium*

Tiny pink waxy flowers hang in clusters from the tips of the many-branched Spreading Dogbane plants often found in colonies or groups in dry soil along the road. The pretty, bell-like blossoms have a slight, pleasant odor. The plant grows up to 2 feet tall, with a reddish, forked stem that has a milky juice similar to that of the Milkweeds. Two long, slender pods, 3–8 inches long, are formed from each little flower.

Although "bane" means "poison," and the name would imply that the plant is poisonous to dogs, there is no evidence that it is of any interest or danger to canines. If you examine the plant closely, you may find a bonus—a coppery, iridescent blue-green insect known as the dogbane beetle.

This and other members of the Dogbane family are more or less poisonous; one, known as the "Ordeal Tree of Madagascar," is reputedly one of the most poisonous plants in the world.

1 Steeplebush (*Spiraea tomentosa*)
2 Steeplebush (*S. tomentosa*)
3 Meadowsweet (*S. alba*)
4 Meadowsweet (*S. alba*)
5 Spreading Dogbane (*Apocynum androsaemifolium*)
6 Spreading Dogbane (*A. androsaemifolium*)

Joe-Pye-Weed (Purple Boneset)—*Eupatorium maculatum*
Ironweed—*Vernonia fasciculata*

A number of the rosy- or purple-flowered species of *Eupatorium* are called Joe-Pye-Weed, differentiated primarily by details of leaves, flower heads, and stems. All have more or less flat clusters of flower heads that are fuzzy or shaggy in appearance when fully open, and the leaves are generally in whorls about the stem. The Joe-Pye-Weeds are all stout, handsome plants of late summer, often in colonies in damp areas and along streambanks, and occasionally reaching a height of 7 feet.

The name "Joe Pye" is variously attributed to an Indian medicine man of the late 1700s who used this herb to cure fevers, or to a Joseph Pye who was recorded as purchasing rum (often used as an ingredient of potions) from a Massachusetts tavern. The leaves of one species, *E. purpureum*, have a vanillalike fragrance, but none of the species, including the white *Eupatorium* BONESET, has any known medicinal value.

You may see a very similar tall plant, known as Ironweed, growing nearby in the same season. *Vernonia fasciculata* is a true Midwesterner. It has tight clusters of flower heads that are a deeper purple than those of the Joe-Pye-Weeds, and the leaves are alternate. The name refers to its tough stem.

Smartweed (Pinkweed)—*Polygonum pensylvanicum*
Water Smartweed—*P. amphibium*

Smartweeds grow just about everywhere. They are so variable, even within the same species, that they grow, tall or sprawling, in dry rocky ground, swamps, ditches, and plowed soil. They may well deserve the appellation "weed," for they do not add much to the landscape, and the tight little pinkish flower clusters in terminal spikes are quite ordinary. They are useful in at least one way, for they produce an abundance of seeds particularly appreciated by game birds.

Among the numerous species, one, sometimes known as Pinkweed, is most readily seen, for it may grow to 4 feet. A shorter, water-loving species, Water Smartweed, has stubby flower clusters which are a deeper pink; a mass at water's edge can be showy and quite attractive. A few of the Smartweeds have an acrid juice which can cause smarting; hence the name given to all, even those which are quite innocuous.

1 Joe-Pye-Weed (*Eupatorium maculatum*)
2 Joe-Pye-Weed (*E. maculatum*)
3 Ironweed (*Vernonia fasciculata*)
4 Smartweed (*Polygonum pensylvanicum*)
5 Smartweed (*P. pensylvanicum*)
6 Water Smartweed (*P. amphibium*)

Birdfoot Violet—*Viola pedata*
Blue Violet—*Viola* sp.
Downy Yellow Violet—*V. pubescens*

Violets, the "footprints of spring," as Edwin Way Teale described them, spring up almost everywhere—roadsides, prairies, streambanks, ditches, woodlands, meadows, and home lawns. They come in shades of purple, blue, yellow, and white; there are about 100 species in the United States alone. All have five petals—two at the top, two side "wings," and a lower one that often serves as a landing place for insects. Although the leaf form varies, a heart-shaped leaf is most typical. Violets are easily recognized, but not as easily identified because they hybridize freely. Both Wisconsin and Illinois have designated the violet as the state flower, though there seems to be some confusion about the species being thus honored.

It may not occur to one to eat such lovely little flowers, but the leaves are high in vitamins A and C, and the blossoms can be candied or even used in a salad for a colorful, if startling, addition to the usual greens.

Violets are often termed "shy" flowers, but that certainly does not apply to the Birdfoot Violet, which forms bold, showy clumps along many dry roadsides and sandy areas in spring. In this species the pansylike flower is held above deeply segmented leaves which resemble the track of a bird's foot. Many consider this to be the most beautiful of the violets.

The Common Blue Violet, *V. papilionacea*, or Butterfly Violet, is perhaps the most familiar. It prefers moister areas. Despite its name, its color varies from deep purple to white tinged with purple.

The Downy Yellow Violet affords an example of how the various species are differentiated. This is one of those which has a leafy stem above the ground with the flower in a leaf axil. The other group, the so-called stemless one, which includes the Birdfoot and the Common Blue Violet, has an underground stem from which the flowers and leaves arise on separate stalks.

1 Birdfoot Violet (*Viola pedata*)
2 Birdfoot Violet (*V. pedata*)
3 Blue Violet (*Viola* sp.)
4 Downy Yellow Violet (*V. pubescens*)

Wild Geranium (Crane's Bill)—*Geranium maculatum*

It is very unlikely that you would name that pretty rosy-lavender flower that embroiders semishady areas along the road in spring a Wild Geranium, for it bears no apparent resemblance to our cultivated Geraniums. It is, in fact, from quite another genus, although of the same family. The name comes from a Greek word referring to the crane, and its other common name, Crane's Bill, is a reference to its odd little seed capsule, which is pointed like the bill of that bird.

The five-petaled 1–1¹/₂-inch flowers, two to four of them, are on forked stalks above a pair of large, deeply lobed leaves. The delicate blossoms belie the rugged nature of this 1–2-foot plant. It has a tough main underground stem, or rhizome, from which new stalks appear year after year, flowering about the same time that trees leaf out. The seed capsule splits open when mature, and the seeds are expelled with sufficient force to shoot them many feet away.

Dame's Rocket (Sweet Rocket, Wandering Lady, Dame's Violet)— *Hesperis matronalis*

Dame's Rocket is a tall, lanky plant of spring and summer that colonizes so readily that you will often find it in large patches. It is an imported old-fashioned garden flower, said to be Marie Antoinette's favorite, which took to the road and flourished. It might be mistaken for a PHLOX until you discover that it has only four petals, not the five of a Phlox; and the long seed pod that develops marks it as a member of the Mustard family. The color ranges from almost white to a deep purple.

The genus name alludes to the fact that the sweet fragrance of Dame's Rocket is heightened in late afternoon. This welcome immigrant has a long blooming period.

1 Wild Geranium (*Geranium maculatum*)
2 Wild Geranium (*G. maculatum*)
3 Wild Geranium seed capsules
4 Dame's Rocket (*Hesperis matronalis*)
5 Dame's Rocket (*H. matronalis*)

Virginia Waterleaf—*Hydrophyllum virginianum*

Although Virginia Waterleaf prefers moist woodlands, it can also be found in damp areas and floodplains along the road. The delicate white to pale lavender flowers are borne in loose clusters on long stalks held high above the leaves. The stamens of the bell-shaped flowers project well beyond the petals, giving the blossoms a fringed or bearded appearance. The leaves are usually mottled with gray or appear to have water stains on them.

Do not pick.

Teasel—*Dipsacus sylvestris*

One of the oddest and most interesting plants that you will find bordering meadows and in waste places along the road is Teasel. This stiff, spiky plant grows 2–7 feet tall, with a prickly 2–4-inch-long "pincushion" at the top of the stem. This pincushion contains tiny lavender flowers which are tucked into closely packed spines and have an odd progression of bloom. They open first in the middle of the head, then progress daily both up and down, sometimes ending up separated into a border at the top and bottom. The leaves are paired, clasping a ridged, barbed stem. The dried egg-shaped heads, with graceful upward-curving bracts at the base, persist into late winter and are a favorite addition to a dried floral arrangement—but one to be handled with gloves. The stout, pronged heads of the related Fuller's Teasel (*D. fullonum*) were once used to raise the nap, or "tease," woollen cloth; hence, the popular name.

1 Virginia Waterleaf (*Hydrophyllum virginianum*)
2 Virginia Waterleaf (*H. virginianum*)
3 Teasel (*Dipsacus sylvestris*)
4 Teasel (*D. sylvestris*)
5 Teasel: dry heads

JULY–SEPTEMBER
Wild Bergamot—*Monarda fistulosa*
JUNE–SEPTEMBER
Oswego Tea (Bee Balm)—*M. didyma*

A spicy fragrance in the air is as much a clue to the presence of Wild Bergamot as the sighting of the shaggy, pale lavender flowers standing tall in dry areas and open woods, often in the company of BLACK-EYED SUSANS, ASTERS, and GOLDENROD. The aroma, opposite leaves, and square stem mark it as a member of the Mint family. One explanation for its name is the resemblance of the scent to that of the aromatic oil pressed from the Italian bergamot orange.

Wild Bergamot's tousled 1–2-inch flower is common and widespread from July on, but its flamboyant relative, Oswego Tea, is more likely to be found in the eastern or southern range of our area, and prefers damp and lightly wooded sites. This scarlet member of the genus *Monarda* is frequently cultivated as a garden flower, and the leaves are still dried for tea, although the brew was more popular with the early colonists, who used it in place of the boycotted English tea. Oswego Indians also flavored meat with the plant, and herb doctors dispensed it as a cure-all. Butterflies and hummingbirds like it, but it has no particular attraction for bees, despite its other common name, Bee Balm.

1 Wild Bergamot (*Monarda fistulosa*), with
  Spotted Knapweed (*Centaurea
  maculosa*) in background
2 Wild Bergamot (*M. fistulosa*)
3 Oswego Tea (*M. didyma*)
4 Oswego Tea (*M. didyma*)

Spotted Knapweed—*Centaurea maculosa*

By midsummer, Spotted Knapweed may be blooming in such profusion that roadsides and open fields appear to have a pale lavender haze. The plants are straggly and many-branched with ragged, fringed flower heads that have a hard knot of bracts at the base of the head. They may, at first glance, be mistaken for THISTLE flower heads, but they lack the prickles of thistles.

All but one of the Knapweed species are aliens; one is cultivated as a familiar garden flower, Bachelor's Button. An individual Spotted Knapweed plant is rather nondescript, but in colonies the plants redeem themselves by the soft color they spread over drab, disturbed ground.

Fireweed (Willow Herb)—*Epilobium angustifolium*

Fireweed appears in large drifts in clearings and charred places, particularly in the northern part of our area. A cosmopolitan plant that flourishes in wood ashes, it sprang up in the bombed areas of London in World War II, giving welcome color to the gray devastation.

The flowers are in a spike, with four mauve petals and eight prominent stamens. The plant is somewhat unusual in that there are seed pods, open flowers, and unopened buds on the stalk at one time. The unopened buds hang down, the blossoms stand out at an angle, and the seed pods are held erect. The leaves are willowlike and alternate. The seed pods split open to release seeds bearing a silky down which are dispersed by the wind. By late summer the 3–6-foot plants are little more than dull stalks tipped with fluff, giving no hint of their earlier colorful array.

1　Spotted Knapweed (*Centaurea maculosa*)
2　Spotted Knapweed (*C. maculosa*)
3　Fireweed (*Epilobium angustifolium*)
4　Fireweed (*E. angustifolium*)
5　Fireweed seedheads

69

Hairy Beardtongue—*Penstemon hirsutus*
MAY–JULY
Foxglove Beardtongue—*P. digitalis*

There are more Beardtongues (*Penstemon* spp.) in the United States than you may want to know about or be able to tell apart. Even the name is a rather obscure reference to a hard-to-see tuft of hairs ("beard") on one of the stamens of the flower. The lipped flowers are a clue to the fact that these plants belong to the Snapdragon family. (On a first quick glance, they may be confused with PHYSOSTEGIA or one of the LOBELIAS.) Hairy Beardtongue, with 1-inch-long magenta-tinged flowers, is the species most apt to be seen along the roadside, for the plant is large and erect. A smaller, white-flowered species, Foxglove Beardtongue, although less easily spotted, is actually more widespread, and is a native prairie plant. Some Penstemons have been developed for growing in the garden, as they are hardy plants and quite insect-free.

Do not pick.

JULY–SEPTEMBER
Creeping Bellflower—*Campanula rapunculoides*
Harebell (Bluebell-of-Scotland)—*C. rotundifolia*

Bellflowers standing 2–3 feet tall often form a clump or ribbon of bloom along the road. This plant, an immigrant from Europe, has gone over the wall and escaped from the garden. The bell-like flowers open all the way up the stem, beginning from the bottom. The term "creeping" comes from the fact that the plant grows from creeping runners.

The Harebell, on the other hand, is truly a wildling and is widespread, often found on rocky roadside shoulders where other vegetation is sparse; it is equally at home in meadows, in sandy areas, and on cliffs. The Harebell is less showy than the Bellflower; the blooms are delicate and airy, nodding on the end of short threadlike stems, singly or in clusters. Although it is often called Bluebell-of-Scotland, its range is almost worldwide, and it is more properly referred to as Harebell to distinguish it from the English Bluebell, which is in another family.

Do not pick.

1 Hairy Beardtongue (*Penstemon hirsutus*)
2 Hairy Beardtongue (*P. hirsutus*)
3 Foxglove Beardtongue (*P. digitalis*)
4 Creeping Bellflower (*Campanula rapunculoides*)
5 Harebell (*C. rotundifolia*)
6 Harebell (*C. rotundifolia*)

Purple Loosestrife (Spiked Loosestrife)—*Lythrum salicaria*

Loosestrife in full, resplendent bloom near the road in ditches, marshes, and river banks is an arresting sight. But this beauty, an import from Europe, is something of a beast to conservationists. Though it is confined to wetlands and damp soil, its aggressive growth has enabled it to take over large areas, crowding out native wildflowers and desirable vegetation needed by wildlife. It arrived in New England sometime in the mid-1800s and gradually spread westward, appearing in our area only in this century.

A number of odd characteristics have enabled this plant to spread and thrive luxuriously. The 2–6-foot spires may contain up to 3,000 flowers in the leaf axils of one stalk, and each flower produces a seed pod with as many as 100 seeds—astronomical productivity for one plant. There are three different kinds of flowers on different plants, with different lengths of styles and stamens, increasing the likelihood of cross-pollination by insects. In addition, the plant can sprout from portions of the root or even from broken stems. The roots form a dense, tough mat that is all but impossible to destroy once the plants are established. The peak blooming period lasts a scant two weeks, and the large stands become a dull rust color, evident then only by their abundance.

A number of other, less conspicuous plants, in this and another unrelated genus (*Lysimachia*), are also commonly called Loosestrife.

Blazing Star (Gayfeather)—*Liatris pycnostachya*

Tall spikes of Blazing Star punctuate meadows, prairies, and roadsides like purple exclamation points from midsummer on. The heads of some are densely packed, with as many as 100 individual flowers, which open from the top down. They are easily recognized as the native genus *Liatris*, for they are stiff, unbranched plants with narrow leaves and a terminal column of tufted short-stemmed or almost stemless flowers. But there are numerous species which also hybridize, making individual identification difficult. The common names, Blazing Star and Gayfeather, are both descriptive and often used interchangeably.

The blooming period is both variable and extended. Some species like damp areas, but the more common ones in our area often make a spectacular show in dry meadows and sandy waysides. A perennial, Blazing Star grows from a corm; Indians once dug and stored the corms for winter use.

Do not pick.

1 Purple Loosestrife (*Lythrum salicaria*)
2 Purple Loosestrife (*L. salicaria*)
3 Blazing Star (*Liatris pycnostachya*)
4 Blazing Star (*L. pycnostachya*)

Hairy Vetch—*Vicia villosa*
MAY—SEPTEMBER
Crown Vetch—*Coronilla varia*

Vetches are sprawling or climbing plants with curling and twisting tendrils on the ends of the leaf segments. Hairy Vetch is one common species that often grows luxuriously along the road, giving a strong blue or purple hue to surrounding greenery when it is in full flower. The blossoms, on stalks growing from the leaf axils, are dense, one-sided clusters which may vary from bi-colored blue and white to pale lavender. The leaves of Vetch are pinnately compound; that is, each one has five to ten pairs of leaflets along a common center stalk.

You will often see masses of Crown Vetch on the cuts of new highways, where it has been planted by road crews to control erosion and stabilize the soil. Crown Vetch has a pretty pink and white pealike flower in a cluster that stands above its foliage.

The Vetches are in the Pea family, and share a common ability to transform nitrogen from the air for the benefit of the plant and the enrichment of the soil after the plant dies.

JUNE—OCTOBER
Bittersweet Nightshade (Climbing Nightshade)—*Solanum dulcamara*

The 1/2-inch purple flowers of Bittersweet Nightshade, with their swept-back petals and distinctive yellow beaks, are less conspicuous than the clusters of green and bright red berries which are often on the plant at the same time. (This plant is no relation to the Bittersweet which is so often used for fall decoration.) The common name comes from the first bitter, then sweet, taste of parts of the plant. Testing this is not recommended, however, for the berries are poisonous, although not fatally so.

The plant was introduced from Europe and was probably spread by bird droppings; it is common now in waste places and roadsides. In the fall, the leaves become an attractive purplish shade. A close relative, called Common or Black Nightshade (*Solanum americanum*), has a similar star-shaped flower, white or purple-tinged; its berries are black.

1 Hairy Vetch (*Vicia villosa*)
2 Hairy Vetch (*V. villosa*)
3 Crown Vetch (*Coronilla varia*)
4 Crown Vetch (*C. varia*)
5 Bittersweet Nightshade (*Solanum dulcamara*)

Heal-All (Self-Heal)—*Prunella vulgaris*
Horsemint (Dotted Mint)—*Monarda punctata*

Heal-All is a robust, square-stemmed little plant, not very attractive but so common and widespread that it is hard to overlook. It thrives in poorly drained soil and sandy places. It was once esteemed as a cure-all remedy, particularly for throat ailments because the flower appears to have a "throat" and "open mouth"—but it actually cures nothing. The dense, terminal flower head, with a few bluish or lavender blossoms at one time, keeps elongating. It is undiscouraged by cutting, and may form a low-growing mat in lawns or other frequently mowed areas.

Another odd plant, Horsemint, is also a member of the Mint family and a relative of WILD BERGAMOT and OSWEGO TEA, but it is unlikely to be noticed as a flower unless examined closely. The blossoms are yellowish and purple-spotted, in tight rosettes about the stem, almost hidden by the white or lilac bracts below them. This grows in open sandy areas, and may take over an abandoned meadow.

1   Heal-All (*Prunella vulgaris*)
2   Heal-All (*P. vulgaris*)
3   Horsemint (*Monarda punctata*)
4   Horsemint (*M. punctata*)

Thistle—*Cirsium* spp.

Thistles are the favorite flower of very few people, and one species—*C. arvense*—is, in fact, outlawed in many states, although the legal standing has scarcely affected it. Thistles are weeds, in any sense of the word, but if you can overlook the prickles, you find some handsome flowers, and large colonies are admittedly a colorful addition to the landscape.

Of the many species which flourish here, most are unwelcome introductions to North America. It takes a dedicated botanist (preferably wearing gloves) to examine the plants for such differentiating features as spines on the stems and bracts, or wool on the underside of the prickly leaves.

The Bull Thistle (*C. vulgare*), the spiniest, often grows to 5 feet or more; it has the largest flower heads, sometimes 2–3 inches across. The Canada Thistle (*C. arvense*)—many branched and with slightly fragrant, smaller flower heads—is the commonest and peskiest. It reproduces both by seed and by rhizomes, so that it is very difficult to control. Its origin is not Canada. Some people believe that it was introduced to the New World in hay transported for the horses of English troops during the Revolutionary War.

The thistle is the Scottish national insignia. It was adopted after barefoot Danish troops, attempting a night attack on a Scotch stronghold, stepped on thistles; their cries of pain awoke the defenders, who were then able to defeat the intruders.

One other thistle admirer is the goldfinch. It is particularly fond of the seeds and delays nest-building until late in the summer, when it gathers quantities of thistledown for lining. Allusions to "light as thistledown" aside, thistledown has no other known use than to aid in dispersing the thistle's seeds.

1   Canada Thistle (*Cirsium arvense*)
2   Field Thistle (*C. discolor*)
3   Bull Thistle (*C. vulgare*)
4   Bull Thistle seedheads and thistledown

79

Aster—*Aster* spp.

The Asters are the flowers that bid farewell to summer; as the Indians say, "They bring in the frost." They are especially appreciated because they often give a splash of color after most other blooms have faded and vegetation is browning.

Identifying the various species accurately will try your patience, for they come in a confusing array of colors and shapes, often varied in hue in the same species, as pictured. Nevertheless, clusters of daisylike ray flowers in late summer are likely to be Asters.

The tall, shaggy clumps of the deep purple New England Aster (*A. novae-angliae*) are the showiest, and stand out on roadside shoulders and ditches from August through late October. This native Aster is the source of many hardy garden varieties. Blooms of other wild Asters range in color from purple and lavender to light blue and white. Many of the white Asters have sparse ray flowers and are coarse in appearance; but one of these, the Frost Aster (*A. pilosus*), has a mass of tiny, 1/4-inch flower heads so thickly clustered that they all but hide the stems and leaves. It coats fields and roadsides with drifts of white, its blooms persisting long into the fall.

1 New England Aster (*Aster novae-angliae*)
2 Asters: varied hues, same species
   (*Aster* sp.)
3 Frost Aster (*A. pilosus*)
4 Flat-topped White Aster (*A. umbellatus*)
5 Smooth Aster (*A. laevis*)

Jacob's Ladder (Greek Valerian)—*Polemonium reptans*

Although Jacob's Ladder, with its pale blue, bell-like flowers, prefers an open woodland setting, it may occasionally be found growing in grassy ditches and along the edges of meadows in late spring. A loose cluster of blossoms appears on short 8–16-inch stems, and the leaves have paired ladderlike leaflets. These pinnate leaves account for the common name, a biblical reference to the ladder to heaven seen by Jacob.

The name Jacob's Ladder is given to several species of *Polemonium*, including a garden variety, but *P. reptans* is most often found in the Midwest. The dainty flowers last for only two weeks or so, but the foliage remains green until frost.

Do not pick.

Forget-Me-Not—*Myosotis scorpioides*

This species of the dainty little sky-blue Forget-Me-Not is a European import, an escapee from early gardens, but it is frequently found now in moist roadside ditches and other wet areas, where it has become naturalized. The tiny flowers are on two curved terminal branches which uncoil as they bloom, and each has a yellow eye. Another wild species, *M. laxa*, is native to North America; it has more minute blossoms, is more branched, and frequently grows in shallow water or on low, wet stream and lake edges.

The flower is considered a symbol of remembrance and loyalty, a favorite of lovers the world over; in fact, the French name is Aimez-moi ("love me"). One story accounting for its English name concerns a young man who was gathering flowers for his sweetheart. He slipped and fell into a deep pool; as he sank, he threw the flowers onto the bank, crying, "Forget me not!" Another legend says that God named all the flowers during Creation, but one small flower could not remember what it was called. Its absentmindedness was forgiven as God whispered, "Forget me not."

1 Jacob's Ladder (*Polemonium reptans*)
2 Jacob's Ladder (*P. reptans*)
3 Forget-Me-Not (*Myosotis scorpioides*)
4 Forget-Me-Not (*M. scorpioides*)

83

Wild Lupine—*Lupinus perennis*

The handsome Wild Lupine, the only species of Lupine native to our area, surely rivals the cultivated garden varieties for stately beauty. The spike of violet-blue pealike flowers stands erect above attractive blue-green palmate leaves with from seven to nine segments. The plant thrives in scrub pine areas, in clearings, and on sandy road banks. By midsummer brown, hairy seedpods stand out on stiff stems above the green leaves and surrounding grasses, soon to twist and turn and "throw" the seeds as much as 15 feet away.

The botanical name comes from *lupus*, Latin for "wolf," because it was believed that the plants "wolfed," or robbed, the soil of nutrients. Actually it does just the opposite, for it is a legume that enriches the soil. *Do not pick.*

Spiderwort (Widow's Tears)—*Tradescantia* sp.

The clear blue or deep bluish-purple cluster of the flowers of Spiderwort makes it easy to see along the road or on the edge of railroad embankments, where it may grow up to 3 feet tall. Each 1½-inch blossom, with its three petals and hairy, blue-bearded stamens, lasts but a day and becomes a sticky jelly that will drop a "tear" when touched in late afternoon. Others open the next day, so there is a continuous succession of bloom until midsummer.

The leaves are long and narrow, with the bases of the two smaller ones encircling the flower cluster. The several species in our area range from white and pink to the typical nearly translucent sky-blue. Spiderworts are often cultivated, and the genus name honors James Tradescant, a gardener of the English royal court. The plant has no known attraction for spiders; the common name, Spiderwort ("spider plant"), is variously attributed to the resemblance of the stamens to the hairy legs of a spider or to the leaf growth habit, which some thought looked like a squatting spider. A very pretty flower has thus been burdened with a rather unattractive name.

1 Wild Lupine (*Lupinus perennis*)
2 Wild Lupine (*L. perennis*)
3 Spiderwort (*Tradescantia* sp.)
4 Spiderwort (*Tradescantia* sp.)

Wild Iris (Blue Flag, Poison Flag)—*Iris versicolor*

The Wild Iris that abounds in moist areas and meadows near the road is easily recognized as the country cousin to the garden Iris. The blue tripartite flower has three petals, three stamens, and a "beard," or crest, on the three petallike sepals. The graceful leaves are grass- or swordlike, each enfolding the next younger leaf. This species has a poisonous rhizome, or root tuber, which was pulverized and used in moderation by the Indians as a cathartic.

The name "flag" comes from the Old English for "rush" or "reed." "Iris," derived from the Greek word for "rainbow," refers to the spectacular colors of many species, and a stylized iris design called fleur-de-lis is an emblem of French royalty.

In addition to the Wild Iris, many cultivated varieties have escaped and turn up in unexpected places along the roadside in June.

Do not pick.

Pickerel Weed—*Pontederia cordata*

Pickerel Weed, in full bloom, is a stunning array of bright blue or lavender flowers in beds in the shallow, quiet water of lakes, ponds, and streams.

The flower stalk rises 1–2 feet above the water, with a sheath at the base of the spike of blossoms. The thick triangular or heart-shaped leaves, equally handsome, are as much as 6 inches across. The plants grow from an underwater rhizome, in habitats favored by pickerel. At one time it was believed that the plant spontaneously bred those fish, a peculiar quality that fishermen would appreciate if only it were true.

1   Wild Iris (*Iris versicolor*)
2   Wild Iris (*I. versicolor*)
3   Pickerel Weed (*Pontederia cordata*)
4   Pickerel Weed (*P. cordata*)

Chicory (Ragged Sailor, Blue Sailor, Coffeeweed)—*Cichorium intybus*

Don't be surprised if you go down a road some bright morning to find it solidly bordered with sky-blue flowers, and then return by the same route later in the day to see nothing but stiff, straggly stalks. Neither your eyes nor your memory have deceived you; the Chicory blossoms you passed earlier have simply finished their lovely show and closed for the day.

The flower heads, with their square-tipped, fringed "petals" (actually ray flowers) as much as 1 1/2–2 inches across, are closely spaced against an almost bare stalk which arises from a rosette of large leaves at the base resembling that of a Dandelion. The young leaves of Chicory, like those of the Dandelion, are sought by some for salad and cooking greens, but the major food value lies in the deep tap root. This is often dried and roasted as an additive to or substitute for coffee. This vigorous root also enables the plant to withstand drought, heat, and mowing, to the despair of highway crews and the delight of travelers.

Chicory's superb shade of blue is rivaled by few common wild flowers; occasionally, though, the blooms are pink or even white. Perhaps because it is usually dismissed as a widespread weed, its beauty is overlooked and no enterprising plant cultivator has tried to domesticate it into a well-behaved garden ornamental. The names Ragged Sailor and Blue Sailor come from a legend about a maiden who waited so long beside the road for the return of her sailor that the gods pitied her and turned her into a patient plant wearing sailor blue.

Flax—*Linum lewisii*

Although Flax might not be considered a common roadside plant, here and there you may come upon a mass of delicate blue flowers in an old meadow, overflowing to the borders of the road—a quite remarkable sight. More than likely, they escaped from cultivation long since, although there are also native species which are yellow, and one which is blue.

The 3/4–1-inch flowers, on a single stem, have five round overlapping petals which fall readily; the bloom is replaced the following day. Best known for its use in making linen and linseed oil, Flax has had other applications in the past; for one, the seeds were mixed with cornmeal as a poultice for mumps. It is also occasionally grown as a garden flower.

1   Chicory (*Cichorium intybus*)
2   Chicory (*C. intybus*)
3   Flax (*Linum lewisii*)
4   Flax (*L. lewisii*)

Leadplant (Devil's Shoestring, Prairie Shoestring)—*Amorpha canescens*

Leadplant, a shrubby, often sprawling plant of prairie and dry road-sides, may attract little notice, for it is neither handsome nor particularly colorful. It has an overall grayish hue, for the leaves have numerous white hairs, giving them a leadlike appearance; and the dense spikes of flowers are muted in color, brightened only by the projecting yellow stamens. The individual flowers, in a closely packed taper, have only a single petal, which is the reason for the genus name, meaning "formless" or "deformed."

The compound leaves have from fifteen to as many as fifty leaflets; on bright, hot days they turn sidewise to avoid the direct rays of the sun. The root of the plant grows deep, making the plant all but impervious to drought. It so resisted the plow of early settlers that they termed it Devil's Shoestring. The rather woody stems may grow to 1/2 inch thick if the plant is left unmowed. It does have some value as range forage. The name Leadplant derives either from the dull color of the leaves or from the fact that the plant sometimes grows on hillsides rich in lead.

Viper's Bugloss (Blueweed, Blue Devil)—*Echium vulgare*

Relatively few blue flowers bloom in dry, open areas in midsummer, so Viper's Bugloss, despite its disagreeable name, is worth watching for. This European immigrant came over early and settled along roadsides and waste areas across much of the United States.

It is a coarse, bristly plant, 1–3 feet tall, with flowers that change colors in a rather surprising way. The buds are pink at first, become an intense blue as they open, and then become purple as they fade. Bright red stamens project from the blossoms, which open one at a time on curled flower branches in the leaf axils.

The plant as a whole is no beauty and is something of a pest to farmers, but it is redeemed by its part-time brilliant color and scarcely deserves its demeaning name. The term "viper" comes from a fancied resemblance of the seed to a serpent's head, with the implication that it would, therefore, cure snakebite and/or discourage reptiles. "Bugloss" is from the Greek for "ox-tongue," which supposedly described the shape of the leaves, and is pronounced "bu-gloss." Neither term seems to have much relevance, but the name is, at least, an easy one to remember.

1 Leadplant (*Amorpha canescens*)
2 Leadplant (*A. canescens*)
3 Viper's Bugloss (*Echium vulgare*)
4 Viper's Bugloss (*E. vulgare*)

91

Hoary Vervain—*Verbena stricta*
Blue Vervain—*V. hastata*

About the best that can be said about Hoary Vervain is that the color of the few insignificant flowers open at any one time on the slim spikes is so intense that a number of plants can turn a dry meadow or highway border a vivid blue-violet. Hoary Vervain is definitely weedy, has a 4–5-foot deep root, and can spread rapidly in a pasture, where, because of its bitter taste, it is left undisturbed by grazing cattle. The leaves have dense hairs and are coarsely toothed, with little or no stalk. The erect flower clusters are often branched. They tend to look as if they were about to burst into full bloom, even when at their peak, for only a small circlet of blossoms appears at one time on the spike that elongates as the flowers ripen from the bottom up.

Another common native species, Blue Vervain, has leaves with a distinct stalk, slenderer flower spires which tend to branch more, and a more intensely blue flower.

The name "vervain" means "sacred bough"; a related species was once used in Greek and Roman ceremonies.

Great Blue Lobelia—*Lobelia siphilitica*
Cardinal Flower (Scarlet Lobelia)—*L. cardinalis*

The Lobelias, of which there are a half dozen species in our range, prefer wet areas but may occasionally be seen growing by the road in damp ditches or on the borders of swamps and lakes. The Great Blue Lobelia is the largest of the blue-flowered species, although the color varies from pale lavender to deep blue. The flower form is distinctive: the petals form a tube and have an upper lip with two lobes and a lower lip with three, often streaked with white, and there is a "beard" on the tip of the stamens. The blossoms ascend a tall spike, each one at the base of a small leaf.

The fiery red Cardinal Flower is also a Lobelia, a beautiful plant that blooms from July to September along streams and wet meadows. The slender spikes are of such an intense scarlet that they are bound to attract attention, even at a distance from the road. The graceful, flaring petals are joined in a deep tube which is accessible primarily to hummingbirds. Although the name presumably refers to the scarlet robes of cardinals of the Roman Catholic church, I prefer to compare it to the flash of red of the cardinal bird. Although once fairly common, Cardinal Flower has been overpicked and is endangered.

Do not pick.

1 Hoary Vervain (*Verbena stricta*)
2 Hoary Vervain (*V. stricta*)
3 Blue Vervain (*V. hastata*)
4 Great Blue Lobelia (*Lobelia siphilitica*)
5 Great Blue Lobelia (*L. siphilitica*)
6 Cardinal Flower (*L. cardinalis*)

Cattail—*Typha latifolia*
Narrow-leaved Cattail—*T. angustifolia*

Cattails are odd, interesting, and conspicuous, for they grow in great colonies in roadside ditches, marshes, and areas of shallow water, easily recognized by their tall spiky leaf blades and peculiar brown heads on 3–7-foot stiff stems.

Their blossoming habit is certainly distinctive. In the spring, a sausagelike cluster of brownish female flowers is formed, and directly above, a light-colored spike of pollen-bearing male flowers appears. After the pollen is shed, the mass of male flowers withers and disappears, leaving only the familiar Cattail cylinder. In the fall this too becomes a fluffy mass of down-bearing fruit, eventually dispersed by wind and rain.

You may also find the Narrow-leaved Cattail (*T. angustifolia*), distinguishable by slenderer leaves and a smaller flower head which will have a bare gap between the male and female clusters. This is the species that is usually sold in florist shops as an ornament. If you pick either kind for a fall arrangement, get the catkins in midseason before they are fully ripe or you will eventually have a very messy drift of fuzz floating about the house.

Cattail down is good insulation and buoyant. The colonists stuffed quilts with it, Indians packed it into cradle boards as diapering, hunters tucked it into boots for warmth, and during World War II it was used as a substitute for kapok in life preservers. Cattail leaves have been woven into long-lasting and comfortable rush chair seats, and, on occasion, the heads, dipped in oil, have served as torches.

The list of Cattail virtues goes on. Cattail colonies provide a valuable habitat for animal life, and few stands of the plant are without red-winged blackbird and muskrat families. And finally, it is edible. The green bloom spikes can be cooked and eaten like corn on the cob; the yellow pollen can be added to batter for pancakes; the root stem sprouts are nutritious as a salad or a cooked vegetable, or pickled; and the root core can be made into flour. Few, if any, wild plants have had such a variety of uses. Euell Gibbons, the well-known plant forager, aptly termed Cattails "the supermarket of the swamp."

1 Cattail (*Typha latifolia*)
2 Cattail (*T. latifolia*): spikes
3 Cattail (*T. latifolia*): seed fluff
4 Narrow-leaved Cattail (*T. angustifolia*)

95

Curly Dock (Yellow Dock, Narrow-leaved Dock)—*Rumex crispus*

To all but those who collect materials for winter floral arrangements, Dock might be considered a rather unattractive weed. The yellow-green flowers in a dense head are insignificant and have no petals. They soon become a mass of winged reddish-brown seeds which often cling to the erect stalk into late winter. The leaves are narrow, wavy, and curled.

Dock's long tap root makes it difficult to eradicate from a field, but for the most part, it prefers unmolested areas along the road and in waste places. It does add a rich brown note to the landscape, and in the past has had many uses beyond the decorative. The young leaves have been used in salads or boiled as a pot herb; home remedies for various ailments have been decocted from it; and the leaves are reputed to relieve the sting of nettles.

MAY–OCTOBER
Asparagus—*Asparagus officinalis*

It is difficult to spot wild Asparagus in the early spring when the tender shoots first poke up through a mat of dead grass, but it's hard to miss it in midsummer, when large feathery masses are a dead giveaway of the presence of the plant—long after it is edible.

After being introduced to North America from the Old World as a vegetable, Asparagus escaped from cultivation to line roadside fence rows over a wide range. The tiny bell-shaped flowers produced in spring are inconspicuous, but in late summer bright red berries festoon the yellow stems.

If you make a mental note of the location and the shape of the old plant stalk, which persists through the winter, you can return for a bountiful harvest in the spring. If you are too late to gather it to eat, you can at least add the delicate greenery to a bouquet of flowers.

1   Curly Dock (*Rumex crispus*)
2   Dock (*Rumex* sp.)
3   Asparagus (*Asparagus officinalis*)
4   Asparagus: fall color and berries

97

JULY–OCTOBER
Common Burdock (Beggar's Buttons, Cockle-Buttons)—*Arctium minus*

Burdock is difficult to avoid or overlook. It is a very large, rank plant that grows by the wayside, in farmyards, and in waste places. Anyone, or anything, passing close to it after the burrs have set carries away prickly mementoes.

Burdock is a biennial. The first year it develops a long root and a 7–8-foot circle of very large leaves somewhat resembling those of rhubarb. (When some large young leaves first appeared on the edge of a neglected garden, I mistakenly advised a novice homesteader to root them out. Those that were overlooked later grew into succulent rhubarb stalks. So much for cursory examination!) The second year the plant sends up a tall stalk with pink or purplish flower heads surrounded by bristly bracts that become burrs with curved hooks; these burrs are said to have been the inspiration to an inventor of a mechanical fastener. After its fulsome growth, the plant—root and all—dies, but the seeds carry on, often borne away on cloth or fur.

There are two common species, *A. minus* and *A. lappa*, distinguished primarily by the length of the stalk of the flower head. Although they share a common prickly nature, do not mistake Burdock for THISTLE or TEASEL.

Admittedly a nuisance, Burdock, like many other weeds, has some virtues. The core of the first-year root growth is edible, and a cultivated variety, called Gobo, is particularly favored by the Japanese for preparation of sukiyaki. The root of the wild species is sometimes sold in markets as Wild Gobo. Medicinal concoctions have been prepared from the young leaves and stalks, as well. And if you have nothing better to do outdoors, you can fashion baskets and chains from the burrs—with great care.

JULY–AUGUST
Foxtail Barley (Squirrel-tail Grass)—*Hordeum jubatum*

The greenery of various grasses, reeds, and sedges blankets roadsides from spring to late fall. Most are considered weeds and are under constant attack by highway mowing machines. Many bear interesting flowers—although the flower heads are seldom thought of as such and are rarely very colorful. One exception is the eye-catching Foxtail Barley, which often grows in streamers or clumps right beside the pavement. It bears long, silky, lavender-tinged plumes that sway gracefully in the breeze, soft to the eye and touch. As the seed head matures and dries to a golden color, the beautiful tails become barbed bristles enabling the seed at the base of each one to be dispersed by clinging to anything that passes close by. The barbs also present a hazard to grazing livestock, by injuring their mouths and throats.

98

1 Burdock (*Arctium minus*): first-year leaves
2 Burdock (*A. minus*): second-year stalk, flowers, and burrs
3 Foxtail Barley (*Hordeum jubatum*)
4 Foxtail Barley (*H. jubatum*)

Bracken Fern (Common Fern, Upland Fern)—*Pteridium aquilinum*
Sweetfern—*Comptonia peregrina*

One generally thinks of Ferns as moist-woodland dwellers, but a few are tolerant of dry areas along the road or open waste places. Ferns can be described as flowerless plants that produce spores instead of seeds.

One of the most common and widely distributed is Bracken Fern. This one is coarser in appearance than most. It grows to 2 feet or more on a stout, erect stem topped by fronds with three primary divisions that spread out rather flatly. When the young, tightly coiled shoots first appear in the spring, they are known as croziers or "fiddleheads." Bracken fiddleheads, as well as those of some other ferns, are edible, with a flavor a bit like asparagus, and you may find them in frozen packages in the supermarket. The term "crozier" indicates a resemblance to a bishop's crozier, or staff. The species name given to the Bracken Fern signifies "eagle wing," and perhaps came to be used because the fronds resemble eagle plumage.

A plant that superficially resembles a Fern, Sweetfern, is not a Fern but a flowering plant, a low-growing bush with a woody stem and slender, lobed leaves, often found in large patches in open, sandy areas. It produces a burrlike fruit containing nutlets, and the twigs and foliage are aromatic—good candidates for sachets. The leaves are also reputed to make a pleasant tea, and deer and grouse feed on the plant.

1   Bracken Fern (*Pteridium aquilinum*)
2   Bracken Fern (*P. aquilinum*)
3   Cinnamon Fern (*Osmunda cinnamomea*):
    fiddleheads
4   Sweetfern (*Comptonia peregrina*)
5   Sweetfern (*C. peregrina*)

Poison Ivy—*Rhus radicans*

If you cannot recognize Poison Ivy, you are well advised to learn how before you have a close encounter. All parts of Poison Ivy contain an oil which causes itching and/or toxic reactions in most people who come into direct contact with it.

Poison Ivy has some pernicious habits: it can take the form of a low-growing plant, of an upright shrub, or of a vine; and it thrives in almost any habitat, including lawns and gardens. Identification is not an entirely simple matter. The first and best clue is the characteristic three leaflets, but even these can vary from smooth-edged to lobed (indented on the edges), can be shiny or dull, and can be of various sizes. All three leaflets are on short, separate stalks joined together at the tip of one longer stalk.

The color changes from light green early in the year, to a deeper green, and then to a vivid orange or wine-red in the fall (at which time one might be tempted to pick the leaves for an autumn decoration, but the results would be quite unpleasant). Clusters of grayish-white berries on bare stems are revealed after the leaves fall, another clue to the plant's whereabouts. Although some birds eat the fruits with no apparent ill effects, the berries should be given a wide berth by humans.

A few other harmless plants have somewhat similar leaves, but if there is any doubt, it is best to obey the injunction, "Leaflets three—Let it be." Poison Ivy certainly rates its classification as a noxious weed.

Do not pick.

1 Poison Ivy (*Rhus radicans*)
2 Poison Ivy (*R. radicans*)
3 Poison Ivy berries
4 Poison Ivy: fall coloration

Off-Road Wildflowers

This section contains photographs and descriptions of a few of our more familiar native wildflowers which you must seek out some distance from a busy highway. Many of them are spring ephemerals: they blossom early and briefly, usually in moist, rich woodlands before the trees have leafed out. The peak of bloom for most is May. They are generally small and delicate, with attractive and unusual shapes and forms; despite their modest size and color, they can be seen easily because there is little distracting greenery about them. A walk in the woods or back country at this season is a rewarding experience.

Hepatica (Liverleaf, Mayflower)—*Hepatica acutiloba*

Hepaticas are one of the first woodland flowers to bloom, a welcome sign that spring has arrived. The ½–1-inch flowers, white, pink, or deep lavender, each on a single 4–9-inch hairy stem, have six, eight, or more petallike sepals with three tiny leaves at the base of the blossoms. The flowers are shy, and you must search for them during their brief blossoming period, but the three-lobed leaves persist throughout the winter. The species pictured has pointed leaves; another, *H. americana,* that may be found in the same locale has more rounded leaves. The old overwintering leaves are often flattened to the ground and are a reddish brown by the time the blooms and the new green leaves appear the next season. Their shape accounts for the name, from *hepaticus,* Latin for "liver," as they were considered to be liver-shaped.

Do not pick.

Bloodroot—*Sanguinaria canadensis*

The radiant white flowers of Bloodroot are wide open on sunny days in early spring, closing at night. The single blossom bud is sheathed at first in a curled-up basal leaf, protected against the cold. The eight- to ten-petaled 1½-inch flower unfurls daily for about a week; the scalloped leaves continue growing large and linger long after the flowers have faded, often forming green patches which do not disappear until midsummer. *Sanguinaria,* "bleeding," refers to the orange-red juice in the stems and roots. The Indians used this as a dye for baskets and as a ceremonial body coloring; early settlers treated various ills with the liquid.

Do not pick.

1. Hepatica (*Hepatica acutiloba*)
2. Hepatica leaves
3. Bloodroot (*Sanguinaria canadensis*): early bloom
4. Bloodroot: full bloom

107

Pasque Flower (Wild Crocus, Windflower)—*Anemone patens*

Pasque Flowers thrust up their soft furry buds and delicate violet, blue, or white 2-inch blossom cups on rocky hillsides and dry, gravelly fields before their own leaves or those of any other plants appear, hugging the ground against the cold. They grow taller as spring advances, amidst a rosette of lacy basal leaves bearing a circle of three unstalked leaves on the blossom stem.

The flowering period is brief but spectacular, as there are usually many flowering stems in a clump, a shimmer of color against the drab background of brown leaves and grass. The petallike sepals fall, and the distinctive feathery seedheads, much like those of PRAIRIE SMOKE, continue to stand out in the still near-dormant surroundings.

Pasque Flower is a Midwesterner that ranges further west; it is the state flower of South Dakota. The common name refers to the time of blooming, often around Easter or Passover; children have also called these plants "goslings," because of the small fuzzy buds.

Do not pick.

Spring Beauty—*Claytonia virginica*

Spring Beauty is appropriately named and often liberally carpets open woodlands. Despite its fragile appearance, it may spread out to rocky roadsides and even thrives occasionally in lawns. The 1/2-inch blossoms, fully open only in bright light, are white or pinkish, with delicate pink veins on five petals in loose clusters on one side of a slender stem. Two narrow, ribbonlike leaves grow partway up the flowering stem, and there may be several such stems from each plant, often reclining or even prostrate on the ground. This plant, too, grows from an underground tuber, or corm, 1/2–2 inches in diameter. The Indians and the early settlers both found it palatable; its flavor has been described as similar to that of boiled chestnuts. Euell Gibbons, the well-known plant forager, has termed the tubers "fairy spuds." The genus name is in honor of an eighteenth-century botanist, John Clayton, who studied many flowers.

Do not pick.

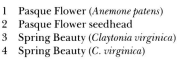

1 Pasque Flower (*Anemone patens*)
2 Pasque Flower seedhead
3 Spring Beauty (*Claytonia virginica*)
4 Spring Beauty (*C. virginica*)

Dutchman's Breeches—*Dicentra cucullaria*
Squirrel Corn—*D. canadensis*

In early spring, the unmistakable winged blossoms of Dutchman's Breeches arch delicately above a mass of feathery foliage, like miniature pairs of yellow-belted Dutch pantaloons strung out to dry. The oddly shaped blossoms have four petals, the outer pair forming the V-shaped inflated spur. Only a few long-tongued insects can reach the nectar within and pollinate the flower.

You may find a very similar plant, Squirrel Corn, growing nearby; the flowers are more heart-shaped and lack the long spurs of Dutchman's Breeches. Squirrel Corn grows from small yellow tubers that resemble grains of yellow corn, but despite the name, they are more likely to be dug up by mice and chipmunks than by squirrels.

Do not pick.

Shooting Star—*Dodecatheon meadia*

This lovely flower is well named; the buds stand erect, and then as the blossom opens, the five swept-back petals trail the "star" or beak of stamens as it points to earth.

Shooting Star was once abundant on the prairies and still grows in open patches along the road, but is now more often found in less accessible or wooded areas. The 1-inch flowers grow at the top of a leafless flowering stalk which arises from a rosette of basal leaves. After its brief burst, the foliage disappears. The flower color ranges from white to pink or magenta.

Do not pick.

1 Dutchman's Breeches (*Dicentra cucullaria*)
2 Dutchman's Breeches (*D. cucullaria*)
3 Squirrel Corn (*D. canadensis*)
4 Shooting Star (*Dodecatheon meadia*)
5 Shooting Star (*D. meadia*)

111

MAY–JUNE
Starflower (Maystar)—*Trientalis borealis*
MAY–JULY
Wild Lily-of-the-Valley (Canada Mayflower, Heart-leaf Lily)—
Maianthemum canadense
APRIL–JUNE
Rue Anemone—*Anemonella thalictroides*
Wood Anemone—*Anemone quinquefolia*

These three little flowers are not related, but have several things in common. They prefer cool, northern woods, and they all bloom in late spring and early summer; on an extended hike, at the same time of year you might find all three in various locales. They are all low-growing plants.

Starflower lives up to its name, with one or more starlike flowers on threadlike stalks above a whorl of shiny pointed leaves. The genus name *Trientalis*, meaning "one-third of a foot," describes its height.

Wild Lily-of-the-Valley has a zigzag stem with two or three clasping heart-shaped terminal leaves and a cluster of tiny star-shaped flowers. It often forms large beds from its creeping underground stems (rhizomes). The greenish berries, which appear in midsummer, persist after the foliage dies and turn a speckled reddish-bronze in the fall. Despite the common name, the plant and flower are quite unlike the garden Lily-of-the-Valley.

Anemonella means "little anemone," and Rue Anemone has several small, delicate blossoms growing on wiry black stems above a whorl of leaves resembling those of MEADOWRUE. It often blooms profusely for several weeks in early spring and then quickly becomes dormant. It is frequently found growing with the Wood Anemone (*Anemone quinquefolia*), which it resembles. The latter, however, has a single similar flower, and the leaves are toothed rather than rounded or lobed.

Do not pick.

112

1   Starflower (*Trientalis borealis*)
2   Wild Lily-of-the-Valley (*Maianthemum canadense*)
3   Rue Anemone (*Anemonella thalictroides*)
4   Rue Anemone (*A. thalictroides*)
5   Wood Anemone (*Anemone quinquefolia*)

113

Bunchberry (Dwarf Cornel)—*Cornus canadensis*

The lovely flowering Dogwood tree of temperate areas has a miniature northern cousin, Bunchberry, which grows only 4–12 inches tall along the edges of cool evergreen forests and moist and acidic open areas. The white, sometimes pinkish 1–1½-inch "flowers" are dwarf but equally showy versions of the blossoms of the Dogwood tree. What appear to be petals are four white bracts with a cluster of true greenish flowers in the center, set off by a circle of four to six leaves, all in a pleasing symmetry.

The plants grow from a woody underground stem, spreading out to form a rich ground cover of green and white. A cluster of berrylike fruits, the "bunchberry," follows, dotting the carpet with glistening red until fall.

Do not pick.

White Baneberry (Doll's Eyes)—*Actaea pachypoda*
Red Baneberry—*A. rubra*

The flower clusters of the Baneberries may be overlooked when they appear in moist woodlands in May or June, but the fruits, called "doll's eyes," stand out prominently in the fall. The two species, White Baneberry (*A. pachypoda*) and Red Baneberry (*A. rubra*), are quite similar, with the major distinction being the thickness of the stem. Both bear glossy "beads"; the White Baneberry fruits are generally white with black centers, which resemble china-doll eyes, and are held high above the foliage on a thick red stalk. The plant's name comes from the poisonous ("baneful") quality of both berries and roots.

1 Bunchberry (*Cornus canadensis*)
2 Bunchberry (*C. canadensis*)
3 Bunchberry fruit
4 Red Baneberry (*Actaea rubra*)
5 White Baneberry (*A. pachypoda*): fruit

APRIL–JUNE
Bellwort (Big Merrybells)—*Uvularia grandiflora*

For a week or so in spring, the dainty Bellwort nestles among the other woodland ephemerals, its 1½–2-inch bell-shaped blossoms nodding shyly on an arched stem which looks as though it pierces the terminal leaf. Although it is sometimes called Merrybells, the plant has a rather woebegone or discouraged appearance. But once it has blossomed, it straightens up and becomes broader, with new leaves. A similar, smaller species in which the stem does not pierce the leaves is called Wild Oats (*U. sessilifolia*).

Do not pick.

MARCH–MAY
Trout Lily (Yellow Dogtooth Violet, Fawn Lily, Adder's Tongue)—
Erythronium americanum
White Trout Lily—*E. albidum*

About the time that the trout season opens, large patches of mottled leaves and nodding yellow flowers appear briefly in woods and damp areas. The plant has many common names; two, Trout Lily and Fawn Lily, are reasonably descriptive, referring either to the time of blossoming—trout season—or to the markings on the leaves, which resemble those on the back of a brook trout or on a fawn. The name Yellow Dogtooth Violet is confusing, for the plant is a lily, not a violet, and "dogtooth" refers to the shape of the small, underground bulb. Adder's Tongue, another name, seems to make very little sense.

The 1-inch flower, with gracefully backward-flaring petals and petal-like sepals, arises on a single stalk from two fleshy, arched basal leaves. Underground branches spread out and produce new bulbs on the ends, but these are slow to develop and may send up but a single leaf and no blossom for several seasons. You will have to be in the right place at the right time to see the plant in blossom, for the flower lasts only a few days, and the leaves soon disappear as well. You may find a less common white species (*E. albidum*) or, in Minnesota and parts of Ontario, a rare pink species (*E. propullans*).

Do not pick.

1   Bellwort (*Uvularia grandiflora*)
2   Bellwort (*U. grandiflora*)
3   Trout Lily (*Erythronium americanum*)
4   Trout Lily (*E. americanum*)
5   White Trout Lily (*E. albidum*)

Yellow Lady's Slipper—*Cypripedium calceolus*
Pink Lady's Slipper (Moccasin Flower)—*C. acaule*

Orchids might be considered the royal family of plants. Then, if you think of them solely as tropical or hothouse flowers, it may come as a surprise to learn that we have many native species, growing in woodlands, bogs, marshes, and sunny clearings. Some genera in this very large family are not particularly attractive and not easily recognized as Orchids, but the Lady's Slippers are large and showy. Indeed, the common name of one, a pink and white beauty, is Showy Lady's Slipper (*C. reginae*), and it is the state flower of Minnesota. Although the Lady's Slippers are far less common now than they were in the past, you can still find them in relatively accessible areas. They are easy to recognize. All Orchids have three petals, one of which is formed into a "lip," or, in the case of the Lady's Slipper, a distinct pouch or "slipper." The odd structural arrangement of this inflated sac makes it an intricate insect trap and assures cross-pollination.

The Yellow Lady's Slipper, of which there are several forms with minor variations, has two greenish or brownish spirally twisted petals on each side of the typical slipper-petal, a greenish-yellow sepal below, and a greenish bract curved over it. There are three to five leaves on the stem, and the plant grows to a height of 2 feet. The Pink Lady's Slipper is called stemless, although there is a visible flower stalk above the two basal leaves; the leaves themselves, however, grow from an underground stem. The pink "moccasin" or slipper has a distinct crease and red veins. Both of these are woodland plants, but they can grow in dry or moist areas. The Showy Lady's Slipper is more likely to be found well off the beaten path, for it prefers cooler bogs and damp woods.

Never pick these orchids; they are slow-growing and easily destroyed.

Do not pick.

118

1 Yellow Lady's Slipper (*Cypripedium calceolus*)
2 Yellow Lady's Slipper (*C. calceolus*)
3 Pink Lady's Slipper (*C. acaule*)

119

Virginia Bluebell (Virginia Cowslip, Lungwort)—*Mertensia virginica*

A colony of Virginia Bluebells in full bloom is a sea of delicate blue on a moist wooded slope or in bottomlands. The 2-inch-long trumpet-shaped flowers are in a nodding two-toned cluster at the tip of an arched stem. Though the buds are pink, the flowers turn china-blue as they open. The leaves, on smooth stems, are large and floppy.

The foliage disappears soon after the seeds are set, leaving no sign of the wave of color that will reappear the following spring. The common names Bluebell and Cowslip are confusing because they are applied to many other flowers, and although the plant grows profusely in some areas of Virginia, it is a more common wildflower of the Midwest. Because it is adaptable and colorful, it is frequently grown in gardens in other areas, as well. The name Lungwort comes from an old belief that the plant would cure lung diseases.

Do not pick.

Blue-eyed Grass—*Sisyrinchium* sp.
Deptford Pink—*Dianthus armeria*

It may take a sharp eye to spot Blue-eyed Grass in a meadow or field as you walk through, but it can be startling to glance down and see tiny, $1/2$-inch blue, white, or purple flowers like bright dots on the tip of grasslike stalks. The name is descriptive but inaccurate, for these are not blossoming grasses at all, but members of the Iris family.

The miniature six-pointed flower is open only for one sunny day; it closes when picked. There are various species of these 4–10-inch plants. You will find them growing singly or in clumps in both wet and dry open areas.

In similar areas, particularly where the ground is dry or disturbed, you may see a vivid spot of deep pink or magenta among the grasses, on a plant that may look very much the same. Deptford Pink (*Dianthus armeria*) is no relation to Blue-eyed Grass. The dainty blossom has five white-spotted petals and narrow leaves close to the stem. The flower cluster is surrounded by small, hairy, leaflike bracts, like those of its cultivated cousin, Sweet William. This is an alien, and the common name refers to its former abundance in fields near Deptford, England.

120

1 Virginia Bluebell (*Mertensia virginica*)
2 Virginia Bluebell (*M. virginica*)
3 Blue-eyed Grass (*Sisyrinchium* sp.)
4 Deptford Pink (*Dianthus armeria*)

Wild Blue Phlox—*Phlox divaricata*
MAY–SEPTEMBER
Prairie Phlox (Downy Phlox)—*P. pilosa*
JULY–OCTOBER
Garden Phlox (Fall Phlox)—*P. paniculata*

Although there are many species of Phlox, the earliest, bluest, and most common in Midwest woodlands and fields is the Wild Blue Phlox. The color is most intense when the plant is growing in lightly shaded damp woods, but it can be found in more open areas as well. The flower cluster of unfurled buds and open blossoms radiates from the tip of a short, rather sticky stem. Wild Blue Phlox is sometimes called Wild Sweet William, but that name is also used for another low-growing species, *P. maculata*, which is more reddish, has spots on the stem, and appears a bit later.

These two, in turn, are followed by two taller Phlox, the Garden Phlox, a much stouter plant with pink-purple flowers that may grow up to 7 feet tall, often an escapee from cultivation, and a shorter wildling of the same hue, Prairie Phlox (*P. pilosa*). The common names vary from one locality to another; the species differ only in minor features; and, to add to the confusion, there are variations of color. Nevertheless, the five-petaled flower and general growth habit make it easy to recognize all these plants as Phlox. Do not, however, mistake Garden Phlox for DAME'S ROCKET: there are only four petals on Dame's Rocket flowers, and it also has the distinctive seed pod of the Mustard family.

1 Wild Blue Phlox (*Phlox divaricata*)
2 Wild Blue Phlox (*P. divaricata*)
3 Prairie Phlox (*P. pilosa*)
4 Prairie Phlox (*P. pilosa*)
5 Garden Phlox (*P. paniculata*)
6 Garden Phlox (*P. paniculata*)

Bottle Gentian (Closed Gentian)—*Gentiana andrewsii*
Fringed Gentian—*G. crinita*

Few flowers are as richly blue as these two Gentians, and they are all the more remarkable because they bloom very late in the season, an unexpected dash of azure among tall grasses and browning vegetation. Although these Gentians seldom grow in masses and prefer moist areas, I have occasionally found the more common Bottle Gentian growing along back roads where I was sorely tempted to put a sign saying, "Please do not mow or spray."

The flowers of Bottle Gentian are like 1–2-inch oval balloons or buds about to open, for the petals are closed or nearly closed at the top. The blossoms are in tight clusters at the top of the stem, above a whorl of leaves and occasionally in the axils of upper leaves. This species is named after Henry Andrews, a nineteenth-century English botanist and artist.

The more elusive Fringed Gentian, considered by some to be our most beautiful American wildflower, is more likely to be found in wet areas, seepage banks, and along stream courses. The swirl of delicately fringed, flaring petals opens only in sunshine, reflecting the blue of an October sky. This biennial plant may disappear altogether from an area where it has once been found; the tiny seeds may have been dispersed elsewhere or have failed to germinate.

The genus name refers to a King Gentius of an ancient country who reportedly discovered the medicinal qualities of the roots of some species.

Do not pick.

1   Bottle Gentian (*Gentiana andrewsii*)
2   Bottle Gentian (*G. andrewsii*)
3   Fringed Gentian (*G. crinita*)
4   Fringed Gentian (*G. crinita*)

Pitcher Plant—*Sarracenia purpurea*

You may pass ten bogs or marshes in northern areas and then, suddenly, find the next one studded with tall leafless spikes topped by the nodding reddish-purple 2-inch blossoms of those fearsome insect traps, the Pitcher Plants. The flowering period is a giveaway to the location of these plants, which are otherwise difficult to see in the sphagnum moss or among the sedges where they grow.

A rosette of heavily veined, pitcher-shaped leaves is at the base of the flowering stalk. Rainwater is caught in the open end and held within the hollow leaves, which are lined with downward-pointing bristles. This combination spells almost certain doom for insects which enter; they cannot crawl back out through the bristles and they fall, exhausted, into the water, where they decompose or are digested. It is generally thought that this provides nutrients which are absorbed by the plant, and as a result, the Pitcher Plant has been termed carnivorous or insect-eating. Some scientists believe, however, that the decaying insects are simply food for the larvae of the flies that pollinate the flower, not food for the plant. In any case, it is an efficient trap. Indians considered the root to be helpful in treating smallpox.

Do not pick.

Bog Laurel (Swamp Laurel, Pale Laurel)—*Kalmia polifolia*

A pink blush hovers over northern bogs and peaty areas in early summer when Bog Laurel comes into bloom. Although you may catch a glimpse of this from the road or from a woodland path, you will have to wade or thrust your way through matted underbrush or spongy moss to see the attractive terminal clusters of blossoms on this low-growing shrub. It's worth the effort. The tiny flowers—miniature versions of those on its better-known relative, the showy Mountain Laurel that grows in the East—have petals joined together in a dainty saucer shape, holding ten dark-tipped, projecting stamens. The narrow, leathery leaves have rolled edges and are white underneath.

Bog Laurel may be found growing with Cottongrass (*Eriophorum* sp.), as pictured; this is a sedge with bolls of white or tawny hairs in the downy heads. Bog Laurel often keeps company with Bog Rosemary (*Andromeda glaucophylla*), as well. The latter is also a low-growing evergreen shrub with pink flowers, but the blossoms are small dangling globes.

1 Pitcher Plant (*Sarracenia purpurea*)
2 Pitcher Plant leaves
3 Bog Laurel (*Kalmia polifolia*) with Cottongrass (*Eriophorum* sp.)
4 Bog Laurel (*K. polifolia*)

Jack-in-the-Pulpit (Indian Turnip)—*Arisaema triphyllum*

This woodland plant, with its very descriptive common name, appears early, but may be overlooked at first because of its predominately green color amidst other lush spring growth. But once spotted, it is easily recognized by the large three-part leaves that guard the odd blossom that is Jack's "pulpit." This is a green or purple-striped funnel-shaped spathe, a leaflike sheath that curves over at the top to provide a canopy over "Jack," the spadix, or flowering spike, within. At the base of this spadix are tiny flowers. "Jack" may go through a sex change. The flowers of young plants are always male (staminate) until sufficient nutrients are stored to support fruitage. Then some become female, or pistillate. Without the proper environment, "he" may be male all his life.

The amount of color in Jack's "pulpit" depends on the amount of light or shade it receives. The plants grow 1–3 feet tall, sometimes as single specimens, sometimes assembled in self-effacing crowds.

Jack-in-the-Pulpit grows from an underground corm, the Indian Turnip of its other common name. This is palatable when properly boiled, but if eaten raw will sting and burn the mouth. In late August, a brilliant cluster of red berries on a tall stalk marks the spot where Jack once held sway over a congregation of WILD GERANIUMS, TRILLIUMS, VIOLETS, and other spring flowers.

Do not pick.

Wild Ginger—*Asarum canadense*

The patches of low-growing, large, heart-shaped leaves that appear on moist forest floors and rocky hillsides in early spring conceal a curious little blossom. The cup-shaped 1½-inch flower of Wild Ginger is dull red, nestled close to the ground at the base of two hairy leaf stalks. The woolly leaves, which grow from an underground stem, or rhizome, stay green until fall. Although Wild Ginger is not related to true ginger, the rhizome has a gingerlike odor and when dried has been used as a substitute for that spice or candied for a flavorful nibble.

Do not pick.

1 Jack-in-the-Pulpit (*Arisaema triphyllum*)
2 Jack-in-the-Pulpit (*A. triphyllum*)
3 Wild Ginger (*Asarum canadense*)
4 Wild Ginger (*A. canadense*)

Glossary
Bibliography
Index

Glossary

Alternate leaves. Single leaves along a stem that are not opposite each other.

Basal. At the base of the stem.

Biennial. A plant that lasts only two years, producing seeds the second year.

Bracts. Green or colored modified leaves, usually at the base of flowers.

Compound leaf. A leaf divided into separate smaller leaflets.

Corm. A bulblike fleshy part of the underground stem.

Disk flowers. Tiny, tubular flowers in the buttonlike center of a flower head, such as the Daisy or Sunflower.

Hip. Rose fruit.

Lobed. Indented on the edge of the leaf, usually with rounded projections.

Perennial. A plant that continues to live from year to year from the stem or root stalk.

Petal. A segment of the flower head, usually flat and brightly colored.

Pinnate leaf. A compound leaf with leaflets along a central stalk.

Pistil. The female organ of a flower, with an ovary, style, and stigma.

Pith. Spongy tissue in the center of the stem.

Pod. A dry fruit that opens when mature.

Opposite leaves. Leaves in pairs, one on each side of the stem.

Ovary. The swollen base of the pistil where seeds develop.

Ovate leaf. An egg-shaped leaf, broader at the base than at the top.

Ray flowers. Flowers that resemble a single petal, arranged around the edge of a circle of disk flowers.

Rhizome. A horizontal underground stem.

Rosette. A cluster of basal leaves, appearing to grow directly out of the ground.

Sedge. A grasslike herb.

Sepal. A small, modified leaf near the edge of a flower, usually green but sometimes resembling a petal.

Spadix. A club-shaped stalk with tiny crowded flowers.

Spathe. A leaflike sheath enfolding the spadix.

Spur. A projection of a part of a flower, usually hollow and often bearing nectar.

Stamen. The male flower organ, bearing pollen.

Stigma. The tip of the pistil that receives pollen grains.

Style. The stalk of the pistil connecting the ovary and stigma.

Taproot. A stout, vertical root.

Umbel. A flower cluster with flower stalks radiating from one point, like ribs of an umbrella.

Whorl. A circle of three or more leaves from one point on a stem.

Bibliography

Field Guides

Courtenay, Booth, and James Hall Zimmerman. *Wildflowers and Weeds.* New York: Van Nostrand Reinhold, 1972.

Niering, William A., and Nancy C. Olmstead. *The Audubon Society Field Guide to North American Wildflowers: Eastern Region.* New York: Alfred A. Knopf, 1979.

Peterson, Roger Tory, and Margaret McKenny. *A Field Guide to Wildflowers of Northeastern and North Central North America.* Boston: Houghton Mifflin, 1968.

Woodward, Carol H., and Howard William Rickett. *Common Wildflowers of the Northeastern United States.* Woodbury, N.Y.: Barron's, 1979.

Regional Guides

Bare, Janet E. *Wildflowers and Weeds of Kansas.* Lawrence: The Regents Press of Kansas, 1979.

Klein, Isabella H. *Wildflowers of Ohio and Adjacent States.* Cleveland: Cleveland Museum of Natural History, 1970.

Lommasson, Robert C. *Nebraska Wildflowers.* Lincoln: University of Nebraska Press, 1973.

Monserud, W., and G. B. Ownbey. *Common Wild Flowers of Minnesota.* Minneapolis: University of Minnesota Press, 1971.

Moyle, John B., and Evelyn W. Moyle. *Northland Wild Flowers: A Guide to the Minnesota Region.* Minneapolis: University of Minnesota Press, 1977.

Smith, Helen V. *Michigan Wild Flowers.* Bloomfield Hills, Mich.: Cranbrook Institute of Science, 1966.

Voss, John, and Virginia S. Eifert. *Illinois Wildflowers.* Springfield: Illinois State Museum, 1978.

Technical References

Fassett, Norman C. *Spring Flora of Wisconsin.* 4th ed., revised by Olive S. Thomson. Madison: University of Wisconsin Press, 1976.

Gleason, H. A. *The New Britton and Brown Illustrated Flora of the Northeastern United States and Canada.* New York: Hafner, 1952.

Rickett, Harold William. *Wild Flowers of the United States: The Northeastern States.* New York: McGraw-Hill, 1966.

Further Reading

Cocannouer, Joseph A. *Weeds, Guardians of the Soil*. New York: Devin-Adair, 1964.

Crockett, Lawrence J. *Wildly Successful Plants. A Handbook of North American Weeds*. New York: Macmillan, 1977.

Crowhurst, Adrienne. *The Weed Cookbook*. New York: Lancer Books, 1972.

Crowhurst, Adrienne. *The Flower Cookbook*. New York: Lancer Books, 1973.

Gibbons, Euell. *Stalking the Wild Asparagus*. New York: David McKay, 1962.

Hersey, Jean. *The Woman's Day Book of Wildflowers*. New York: Simon and Schuster, 1976.

Klimas, John E., and James A. Cunningham. *Wildflowers of Eastern America*. New York: Alfred A. Knopf, 1974.

Line, Les, and Walter Henricks Hodge. *The Audubon Society Book of Wildflowers*. New York: Harry N. Abrams, 1978.

Rickett, H. W. *Wildflowers of America*. New York: Crown, 1953.

Sperka, Marie. *Growing Wildflowers: A Gardener's Guide*. New York: Harper & Row, 1973.

Index

THE FIRST section of the index lists, by color, flowers which are described or pictured in color sections other than their own.
Numbers in boldface type refer to pages containing photographs.

141